500

Tips for

School

Improvement

HELEN HORNE AND SALLY BROWN

KOGAN
PAGE

500 Tips from Kogan Page

500 Computing Tips for Teachers and Lecturers, Phil Race and Steve McDowell
500 Tips for Research Students, Sally Brown, Liz McDowell and Phil Race
500 Tips for School Improvement, Helen Horne and Sally Brown
500 Tips for Teachers, Sally Brown, Carolyn Earlam and Phil Race
500 Tips for Trainers, Phil Race and Brenda Smith
500 Tips for Tutors, Phil Race and Sally Brown
500 Tips on Assessment, Sally Brown, Phil Race and Brenda Smith

First published in 1997

Kogan Page Limited
120 Pentonville Road
London N1 9JN
and
22883 Quicksilver Drive
Stirling, VA 20166, USA

British Library Cataloguing in Publication Data

A CIP record for this book is available from the British Library.

ISBN 0 7494 2230 0

Typeset by Jo Brereton, Primary Focus, Haslington, Cheshire
Printed and bound in Great Britain by Biddles Ltd, Guildford and King's Lynn

Contents

How To Use This Book

We don't imagine for a moment that any reader of a book such as this would wish to read from start to finish, taking on board each and every tip we have written! For a start, you are likely to have already put into practice many, or most, of the ideas we suggest. It is the ideas you may not have thought of yet that are the point of this book. There are several ways in which this book can be used, and we invite you to experiment with any or all, to help you get the most from it. Here are some suggestions.

- **An agenda for group discussions.** When you have a group of colleagues getting together to discuss developments and problems, you might find that suggestions we have made under one or more topics could provide you with a starting point for your discussions.

- **As pre-reading before meetings.** When you have a meeting coming up where planned improvements are to be discussed, you might find it useful to circulate notes taken from parts of the book as preparation, to get everyone thinking about the issues to be debated.

- **As a companion for new staff.** A book such as this can be the basis of a personal profile of development. New colleagues may be able to draw many straightforward things from this book, without having to wait for time to be available to discuss ideas with more experienced colleagues. This can make face-to-face discussion time all the more valuable, as it can be used for the most important issues rather than routine ones.

- **As a companion for experienced staff.** It's all too easy to be so busy doing the job, that time to think about other ways of doing it is hard to find. A handy source of ideas comes in useful for busy people.

- **As an introduction for school Governors.** Scanning this book should provide Governors who may not already be familiar with the day-to-day business of running a school with a broad perspective of what is involved. This may help them to be as supportive as possible when changes and developments are planned and introduced.

- **As a source of reference for parents.** In particular, parents taking leading roles in Parent–Teacher Associations may find parts of this book useful, helping them to see what is involved in planning and implementing school improvements.

- **As a dip-in, start-anywhere resource.** This is not the sort of book to work through in a linear way. We hope that the contents pages and index will help you to pinpoint areas of the book that are most relevant to you in the context of your own day-to-day work.

- **As a starting point for school policy decisions.** When improvements are being introduced, it is important that everyone feels a sense of ownership of the plans that have been made. The ideas in this book might provide a suitable background framework against which detailed plans for the introduction and implementation of school improvements could be developed.

We hope these suggestions are useful starting points, and that you will find even more ways of putting to use the ideas in this book.

Acknowledgements

We would like to thank a number of people who have helped us especially in writing this book. First of all, our gratitude goes to Carolyn Earlam, Myles Easterby, Sue Gallagher, John Harrold and Mike Gibbons, who gave us feedback at the pilot stage, Charlie Egerton and Janet Simpson who contributed ideas for the book, and Phil Race for his boundless patience and support in drafting and preparing the final manuscript of the book.

Chapter 1 Managing School Improvement

If school improvement is to be effective, it is essential that all stages of the process are well planned and well managed. We begin with some suggestions on initiating school improvement, in particular relating to the collection of relevant data to ensure that planned improvements start with the present position of the school, and are therefore likely to be realistic rather than fantasies. Data collection is something that can be done a bit at a time, and once a good database is established it requires minimal time and effort to keep it updated as a normal process in the everyday operation of the school, especially if data collection is targeted and good use is made of appropriate IT.

School improvement is about change. It is human nature to be wary of change and even hostile to it. Our next set of suggestions concentrates on ways of making change more palatable, and trying to generate a widespread feeling of ownership regarding the most important changes to be implemented.

We next turn to the use of a 'Statement of Principles' as a way of not only delineating the mission of the school, but also serving as a sound basis for the implementation of improvements. It is important that each particular school's statement highlights their individual priorities, taking into account the context, locality and ethos of the school.

A 'whole school review' sounds a daunting prospect, but when it is based on data that is already largely available, and firmly linked to agreed principles, it becomes much more straightforward. We provide suggestions as to how to go about such a review.

Next, we extend the principles of whole school reviewing to whole school planning. It is important to make planning a logical and natural continuation of data collection and the processes of arriving at the mission of the school. We next extend the discussion to the formulation of management policies and structures, to set a firm foundation for the detailed planning and implementation of improvements. We also detail how to set about prioritising needs and setting realistic targets.

Whole books are available on managing departments! We end Chapter 1 by presenting just ten key suggestions regarding how best to prioritise good management principles within the context of managing the learning in a school department. There is no doubt that the effectiveness of the design, and implementation, of a programme of school improvement depends vitally on the way that these processes are managed, both at whole school level and departmental level.

1

Initiating school improvement

Before a school can initiate a school improvement programme, there needs to be a clear view of the starting position, so that added value can be readily perceived. This first section aims to suggest ways in which this can be done effectively and efficiently without making unnecessary additional work for those involved.

1 **Establish a baseline from which to improve.** You will need to know a lot about your school at the outset so that you can note successes and achievements, identify any problems and list the issues that are central for your school.

2 **Create a profile of the school.** Just as a builder surveys a site before building can commence, so those planning to undertake school improvement will need to set out baseline measurements of the fundamentals so there is something to build up from. The more accurate the picture you create, the more likely it is that you will not only be able to bring about improvement but also you will be able to see clearly where this has happened.

3 **Build your team.** Choose those who will be doing the baseline profile carefully; don't just go for the most senior staff. You may get a fresher and more accurate view if you get snapshots from different perspectives. Put together a small group of capable, sensitive and clear-sighted people, who are not already overburdened with work.

4 **Slice the school in different ways.** Try to get not just a vision of the school vertically from a hierarchic point of view, but also slice laterally across departments and year groups so the picture is as complete as possible. This also helps to establish across the whole school a sense of ownership of the changes that may be planned.

5   **Start with data that is easy to collect.** You are likely already to have data on such things as: entry performance; exam results; how many pupils you have excluded from school in the last five years; how many pupils have gone on to higher education and where; what have been the ultimate career destinations of those who get jobs; what proportion of ex-pupils are unemployed and so on, so start with data already available.

6   **Check your data**. Circulate it among people in the school who are familiar with the territory so they can check its accuracy and advise the team when it is off-beam.

7   **Analyse your data.** See what you can extrapolate, for example, on how well girls and boys are performing respectively, or whether there are any noticeable differences between different ethnic groups' performances. Check out which subject areas are performing better than others, and where your school's strengths and weaknesses lie.

8   **Look for gaps in your data.** Ask the difficult questions and explore areas where it is not as easy to get access to the information as you wish. Knowing that you don't know something is often useful in building up a true picture of the school and gives you new avenues for exploration.

9   **Describe your data in easily understandable ways.** Make use of the whole range of ways of explaining your data and helping people to make sense of it, including graphs, charts, tables, databases and meaningful descriptions in words!

10 **Make it easy to update your information.** Find ways of continuously monitoring and adding to your information base so you are able to spot trends as they emerge. The best way to make school improvement a normal part of the development agenda is for the process to be embedded in the everyday functioning of the school, and that starts with making the collection and updating of relevant information an unexceptional process.

2

Managing change

Individuals often resist change. Staff can be more concerned about how the change will affect them individually and personally, than about the benefits of any school improvement programme. It is therefore essential to try to translate these negative feelings into positive action by effective management of the process.

1   **Expect resistance and look for ways to counter it.** Most people hate change especially when they believe themselves to be currently working effectively and well (even if they are not). Change can be threatening, but can be a relief sometimes. People tend to hate change when they think their weaknesses will be exposed by it (in which case, support is needed) or when they feel it is change for the sake of change (which is understandable).

2   **Encourage staff to be part of the change rather than subject to it.** Wide consultation is the key to getting people to take ownership. Nobody likes to feel they are having changes thrust upon them and staff are certain to resent change if they don't see the point of it. Where possible, get staff to suggest ways of making the changes themselves. Adopt a genuinely flexible approach if they come up with useful ideas that were not part of the original plan.

3   **Prompt discussion of the reasons for change.** Everyone is more likely to accept change if they are able to recognise what is wrong with the status quo. Golden ages are rarely permanent anywhere other than in people's minds, and a recognition that there are flaws in the current system is often the first stage towards commitment to new models of action.

4   **Counter anxieties about the rate of change.** Sometimes it is necessary to take action fast to prevent disaster (as is often the case when there are financial implications). However, very rapid change can be alarming, especially if people don't feel fully informed, so keep those involved briefed as far as possible as the new situation emerges, without being alarmist.

5   **Treat people with courtesy and respect.** The way people react to change often depends to a great extent on the way that information is handled. If decisions are imparted without opportunities for discussion, or if supposed consultation is perceived as a sham, then resistance will be maximised.

6   **Prepare people for change.** As far as circumstances permit, allow plenty of time for people to voice their fears and reassure them about the unrealistic ones. Be straight with colleagues about the fears that are justified and emphasise ways in which the worst effects are ameliorated. Emphasise the positive aspects of what is being planned and explain who will benefit and how, focusing always on the ultimate good of the school.

7   **Support staff when they are feeling insecure.** Prevent people from feeling they are losing face through change. Recognise that they might feel personally undermined if their comfort zone is being threatened.

8   **Help staff to believe they can cope with change.** The fear of the unknown often leads to a fear of failure, which can be self-fulfilling. Individuals are often frightened to expose their own inadequacies, so they will block change as a self-defence mechanism against exposure. Reassure them of their value and their place in the process.

9   **Emphasise that change doesn't necessarily involve more work.** In fact, some changes of practice can actually make life easier, but staff will need to be convinced of this before they will believe it, so make the case clearly and logically.

10 **Help staff to see the big picture.** Work at helping staff to refocus from their individual perspectives to the universal, seeing potential change as being for the benefit of the whole school. Encourage them to be open to alternatives where these can be seen for the general good.

3

Arriving at a Statement of Principles

A Statement of Principles is a mission statement that sets out the educational goals of a particular school, which have been agreed as desirable. All staff need to be involved in the discussion so that a shared and achievable vision can be agreed by all staff. Building a whole school perspective to which everyone subscribes enables the Statements of Principles to be identified. From such a statement, plans, policies and structures can be derived. In order to do this, it is necessary for management teams to achieve each of the following stages.

1   **Involve all concerned.** When arriving at a Statement of Principles, it is a good idea to consult all those who have an interest in the school: staff, pupils, parents, governors and the wider community. You can do this by holding large-scale consultation sessions, small focus group discussions and paper methods such as circulating draft papers for comment and asking specific questions in a questionnaire.

2   **Learn to ask the right questions.** This is necessary to identify strengths and weaknesses of the school which can be used as a basis for decision making and planning. Look for the less than obvious ones as well as the givens, and use other people to help you generate them. Ask, 'What is it we need to know about the school?' and use this to help you build your profile.

3   **Draw on the experience of others.** Have a look at the Statements of Principles produced by other schools whose ethos you respect. Recycling is an excellent pedagogic principle! Select from them the parts that seem to fit your school and circulate them for discussion and modification as appropriate.

4   **Ensure that planning is rooted in the principles agreed.** All further planning, whether whole school, departmental or individual, can then be done within the context of the agreed Statement of Principles.

5 **Nurture this vision.** Perhaps one of the most significant roles of the headteacher is to nurture the overall vision of the school. At whole staff meetings aspects of the Statements of Principles can be discussed.

6 **Constant reinforcements are necessary and desirable.** The vision of the school should pervade the atmosphere. The whole environment should reflect the attitudes and values of the school.

7 **Think aloud.** Senior management can reinforce the Statements of Principles by often thinking aloud about policy matters as they discuss issues with colleagues in an informal way.

8 **Marry internal priorities with external forces.** Having clear Statements of Principles allows a school to translate external policy decisions, from whatever source, into needs at school level.

9 **Take a proactive stance.** Having Statements of Principles allows a school to have a proactive attitude to change rather than a reactive crisis management approach. It is not a good idea to stumble along waiting to be hit by a problem; it is far better to plan for contingencies in advance.

10 **Express aspirations.** Having a policy statement enables a school to publicise its aspirations and have a written document of intent for all concerned in the school and its welfare in the environment.

4

Undertaking a whole school review

Once a school has devised a mission and Statement of Principles, it can then produce developmental plans for use throughout the school to provide specific targets which can then be translated into action. In order to arrive at meaningful, specific and measurable targets, it is initially often helpful to carry out a whole school review (or curriculum audit). Once systems have been set up, school review should become an ongoing process, rather than just a one-off event.

1   **Carry out a curriculum audit.** This will enable the school to assess its current curriculum provision and pupil access to it. This audit will then provide helpful benchmarks when devising a whole school development plan.

2   **Do a SWOT analysis**. This should look at the strengths of the school, its weaknesses, the opportunities for development and any threats to the success of your plans for improvement. This will help you know what you need to build on, what needs remediation, which directions it will be fruitful to follow and what you will need to look out for so your plans are not stalled.

3   **Check that actual provision matches the planned curriculum.** Also take into account any statutory obligations as well as the curriculum provision that the school wishes to provide in relation to the Statements of Principles agreed by the staff.

4   **Locate gaps and overlaps.** Conducting a curriculum audit enables the school to see if there is any shortfall between intention and reality. Similarly, when a school conducts an audit, it often finds that several departments are covering the same curriculum areas, each unaware of the other's work. This can mean an unnecessary duplication of resources.

5   **Analyse provision in terms of curriculum objectives.** This is important at the various Key Stages of the National Curriculum. It is important that the school meets its statutory needs, before it allows itself freedom to develop its own agenda in areas of specialism.

6   **Assess how much time is apportioned to each subject area.** In some schools, for example, a disproportionate number of hours is spent teaching, say, maths, where there has historically been a very strong Head of Mathematics. After review, a school can then reassess its priorities for change and development.

7   **Review resource provision.** A school needs regularly and critically to look at its resources both in terms of staff and its more flexible disposable budget. Schools will then need to prioritise the use of all kinds of resources in the light of its Statement of Principles.

8   **Review the previous year's resource allocations.** Decide how effective and efficient this has been, and analyse the basis on which previous decisions were made. It will then be possible to reconsider allocations and to plan ahead accordingly from a well-informed point of view.

9   **Make sure that the plan determines the spending of resources rather than letting the resources determine the plan.** Ensure that decisions are made systematically to fit in with the whole school plan, rather than letting the money be allocated and then deciding how to spend it.

10 **Derive future development goals from your current school review.** Forward planning can then be based on realistic data rather than inspired guesswork.

5

Developing whole school planning

The nearer that we can bring the objectives of individuals in an institution to the objectives of the institution itself, the more likely we are to succeed. Developing a whole school plan that really can effect change relies on everyone pulling together towards the same goal. These tips are designed to help you think about how to achieve this.

1   **Involve all staff in the process.** Getting everyone onboard is possibly more important than the plans themselves. Every member of staff needs to feel involved in the process of developing school policies as, without this involvement, they will feel no ownership of the process and will therefore be able to detach themselves from any outcomes they find uncomfortable.

2   **Set up a structure to enable all staff to be included.** In small schools this is easier as staff meetings can be more intimate and discussions can be meaningful. In a large secondary school, communication is usually more difficult. Some form of consultation structure and process will need to be devised so that everyone has the chance to be heard and to add to the debate constructively. Those who feel themselves to be marginalised by the process can have an adverse effect on the outcome.

3   **Build a vision of what you are trying to achieve.** This is not a romantic idea but a basic philosophy that fits the school and expresses the essence of what you are aiming for. This vision can successfully be guided by a single individual, but where this is the case, the school will need to be convinced of the value and importance of it even more than when the vision is collectively achieved.

4   **Write a mission statement.** The educational goals of any school reflect its particular mission. It represents what that school regards as desirable and provides a reference point for all staff and parents. Mission statements

are usually best when they are brief, to the point and clearly identifiable with the school involved, rather than written in high flown or jargonistic language with little relevance to the local context.

5   **Set priorities.** Once a shared vision is established and people know what they are aiming for, it is easier to prioritise the targets and goals that are being set and work out which ones are to be worked towards first.

6   **Plan objectives.** This needs to be done to ensure that the priorities can be achieved. Generalised goals are not enough: there need to be a set of objectives that can be shared among all the stakeholders who can therefore participate in their putting into practice.

7   **Don't set the plan in tablets of stone!** This tends to create a straitjacket, rather than produce a vehicle for change and development. School planning should be a continuous process of planning and replanning. It needs to be a cyclical process, with the flexibility to respond rapidly and appropriately to changing circumstances.

8   **Promote collaboration.** Make practical efforts to involve not only all staff but also pupils and the community in planning activities. This will clearly give a broader vision and help to build a cohesive environment. It will also make it more likely that goals will be achieved.

9   **Link vision building and planning activities.** Mission statements should not be seen as simply bits of paper that lie in drawers and have been compiled merely as an OFSTED imperative. Use one to inform the other and regularly check routine activities to ensure that they match the school's mission.

10   **Be willing to learn by making mistakes.** Don't feel constrained by the plans, experiment with ideas and strategies. If they are not successful, try something else.

6

Target-setting

In order to raise standards and improve learning it is essential to set targets for improvement. The effective management of a school involves setting targets and using suitable benchmarks to raise the performance of both teachers and pupils. National testing is now firmly established, so it is possible to set targets based on Key Stage test results, as well as GCSE and A-level. From these data schools can monitor trends and devise suitably stretching targets for action.

1   **Targets should be stretching.** Local education authorities will have a key role in working with schools to set suitably challenging targets. They will also provide forums to link national targets to local ones. Schools should use the data from such indicators as Key Stage test results and OFSTED inspection analysis to set targets that aim to extend performance rather than just consolidate it. Stretching targets encourage all staff to provide pupils with activities aimed at improving performance.

2   **Use software to analyse results.** This is important, especially as the amount of information available for analysis will grow rapidly. Packages are available to help you compare achievement against prediction for individual students, cohorts of students and for teachers themselves. This baseline data will help you continuously monitor performance, spot gaps and make plans accordingly. Use examples of good practice to help, such as *Setting Targets to Improve Standards* (OFSTED/DfEE).

3   **Ensure that targets can be accurately measured.** The use of appropriate IT will enable data thus derived to help schools ask, 'What more should we aim to achieve this year?' and base their targets on the realistic and agreed level of improvement. Comparative data will then be available for use in examining performance against locally and nationally set targets.

4   **Monitor performance against deadlines.** If a timescale for action is agreed, it will allow schools to review progress and modify or update the targets to improve performance (or reasonably to determine the constraints that prevented that achievement).

5   **Make use of a range of information.** When a school asks itself how well it should be doing, it needs to have appropriate external benchmarks against which to determine realistic targets for improvement. National Curriculum performance tables and OFSTED inspection documents will provide useful starting points.

6   **Compare like with like.** Although the essentially school-based nature of target-setting is likely to remain, don't allow complacency to permeate the school if your performance seems above average.

7   **Work with what you've got.** If your school already has high achievements, set targets that point to further progress. Similarly, don't be despondent if your results are below average: use the information available to plan for realistic development. Make sure you compare results with a similar type of school in a similar locality using appropriate statistical indicators.

8   **Produce an annual report.** This should summarise the progress of an individual school towards national targets. Incremental progress can then be planned and, as your school comes closer to targets and performance rises, it will be possible in subsequent years to set higher targets.

9   **Take local and regional factors into account when setting targets.** It is important to set goals in relation to your particular type of school and its locality, since individual schools need different targets. Ensure yours are realistic and feasible in the context of your school.

10   **Base target-setting on the average results achieved.** It can be problematic to base targets on the percentage of pupils obtaining certain grades. This leads to an emphasis on boosting performance on selective categories rather than across the board. It is therefore beneficial to base performance indicators in terms of the average results achieved.

11   **Use data from more than one year.** Don't simply rely on a single set of statistics, as they could be idiosyncratic and unrepresentative. Performance can vary due to intakes fluctuating from year to year, so targets should take this into account.

12   **Use what is available to you.** Guidance will be given to schools from local authorities and other agencies as to how to establish the most effective kinds of school improvement. In some cases funding may be available. Use whatever resources you can to maximise effectiveness.

13   **Be responsive to changing circumstances.** Be sufficiently flexible to change targets as circumstances change. Avoid being stuck with targets that are no longer meaningful.

7

Devising management policies and structures

A consistent philosophy across all aspects of the organisation is a key feature of any successful school. To achieve maximum effectiveness in performance, a school needs to help individuals to develop within the appropriate frameworks and, at the same time, to use those skills to help the institution as a whole to achieve its goal of raising standards. To do this, it is vital that management policies and structures will achieve the following goals.

1   **Have a consistent approach across the whole school.** Everyone needs to recognise and adopt the school's philosophy, which must filter through all aspects of planning, both at whole school level and the departmental level. If different groups within a school have different philosophies, they can end up working against each other's interests.

2   **Respond to individuals' initiatives.** A school is made up of many individuals whose skills need to be channelled into the overall improvement of the schools. Staff must be given the confidence to try new ideas and develop initiatives in a supported environment and an appropriate structure.

3   **Delegate responsibility.** Delegate to the best person to do the task, chosen on relevant qualities, rather than necessarily the next person up or down in the hierarchy. This gives everyone a chance to demonstrate their skills and initiative. It builds confidence and helps motivation.

4   **Devise a democratic form of decision making.** Schools with active but democratic leadership tend to handle change more comfortably than where an autocratic or didactic mode of leadership is adopted. People like to feel valued and heard.

5   **Have expectations of improvement.** Encourage staff to be comfortable with the idea of change or growth. If this sends shivers down spines, there will be little growth in the school and little school improvement.

6   **Trust people.** Most members of staff take a pride in their work and in their institution. Therefore, it makes sense to trust that they too want the best for pupils in the same way as the management. If this is not felt, you may need to look again at the Statement of Principles and consider whether it needs revision and discussion.

7   **Link theory and practice.** Make sure that the ideals decided in the Statement of Principles are pragmatically organised. Having carried out curriculum audits and other evaluation techniques, it is then possible to link a practical use of resources to the ideals agreed by staff.

8   **Manage people as well as resources.** Management need to avoid being overwhelmed by the process of allocation of resources, neglecting the 'people' issues. Staff are the most costly but valuable resource that a school possesses, so managing people effectively as well as sympathetically is of vital importance. Clarify roles and responsibilities through clear job descriptions.

9   **Encourage an 'open door' policy** – an open door not only to staff but also to parents. Parents are a valuable resource to be harnessed in the process of continual improvement. Make it possible for them to be involved in all kinds of activities such as visits, Parent–Teacher Associations and fundraising, as well as helping in the classrooms.

8
Managing learning within departments

Heads of departments, like other managers, can too often see their role as managing resources rather than managing people. Setting priorities, reviewing and evaluation are just as much the responsibility of middle management as they are of every individual in the school. Just as the school needs whole school action plans to help plan and coordinate activities, so must there be departmental planning to manage learning within the departments. Whole school and subject development must work together so that goals and targets are integrated. To do this, departmental managers need to:

1 **Help their departments to develop unified goals within subject areas.** It is important to marry the approaches of any given department to the approach of the whole school at the same time as putting their own particular spin on the overall plan.

2 **Establish clear priorities for the department.** These should work within the context of an agreed Statement of Principles for the school as a whole and should enable the department to agree subject-specific priorities. Departmental priorities will also take into account individual appraisal targets, so that personal and professional development can be targeted toward both the department's and the school's needs.

3 **Be precise in costing.** Effective management of a departmental budget is essential to maximise the use of scarce resources. Costing priorities within an agreed policy makes budgetary decisions easier. Any funding available can then be spent to best effect according to identified needs.

4 **Build in deadlines for action within the department.** Any initiatives for change and development should have integral timescales for completion and evaluation. If these are not agreed and monitored, so that all staff are aware of schedules and deadlines, things tend to drag on and little improvement occurs.

5   **Share and name responsibilities.** Make clear who is committed to doing what, rather than giving tasks to loosely defined teams. Avoid, as far as possible, putting 'Everyone' or 'All interested' alongside action lists, as this tends to mean no one feels personally responsible for seeing that the job is done. Make sure that there is a written record of commitments to tasks, so that accountability is assured.

6   **Identify clear and measurable outcomes.** These should be expressed in terms of pupils' improved learning and performance. Once you have established a benchmark for existing performance, it should be possible to identify what improvements are to be achieved by a given date (or at least to review progress to date).

7   **Construct schemes of work.** Use the criteria laid down by the curriculum of the Key Stages and translate and incorporate them to fit the needs of the school. Then you can construct schemes of work that enable pupils to achieve the best results possible.

8   **Monitor progress between the Key Stages.** Use a range of evaluative skills, standardisation meetings and records to monitor the continuity of progress between the Key Stages. This will help you to check the progress made by individuals and groups of pupils.

9   **Devise regular, subject-specific staff development.** Use regular departmental meetings to enable colleagues to share ideas about improving pupil achievement as well as more elaborate initiatives to develop team teaching or to devise new schemes of work.

10 **Monitor inservice education and training (INSET) within departments.** The time spent on staff development within a department and the way it is used must be reviewed periodically. Priorities need to be constantly drawn to ensure the maximum use of all the resources in a department.

Chapter 2 Effective Teaching And Learning

Effective teaching and learning processes do not just happen – they are the product of careful planning and design. We start this chapter by giving suggestions on a wide range of aspects of planning, ranging from clarifying curriculum aims, and the use of resources, to the development of the whole school planning and its monitoring and progression.

We turn our attention next to teaching and learning strategies, and in particular, how these can be tuned to pupils' own expectations, experience and developing expertise. It is useful to explore how much pupils can be involved in the design of the delivery of curriculum. Involvement can give them an increased sense of motivation and purpose.

Next we offer some suggestions regarding the use of information technology in the classroom. Many teachers are extremely computer-literate, and will need no advice on how best to do this. However, there are others who, for one reason or another, have not had the occasion or need to develop computer skills, and it is to these that our suggestions in this section are offered. (For anyone requiring many more tips on choosing and using computers in teaching and learning, we refer readers to *500 Computing Tips for Teachers and Lecturers* by Phil Race and Steve McDowell, Kogan Page, 1996.)

Our suggestions on 'Improving classroom organisation and management' necessarily overlap with many other parts of this book. However, we concentrate here on ways of making the classroom a well-organised and appropriate learning environment, conducive to effective learning and participation by pupils, and more suitable for the performance of teaching and learning.

Our next set of suggestions is on 'Managing relationships', and sets out some straightforward but important principles for ensuring that you maintain your credibility with pupils and earn their respect. Such credibility and respect are cornerstones on which school improvements can be founded.

Variety is the spice of effective learning (and teaching). We continue with some suggestions regarding the variety that you can plan into teaching and learning processes in your classroom. We continue this theme with suggestions about ensuring that pupils are involved in their learning activities, in ways that will lead to improving motivation. When pupils really want to do something, the chances that they will learn from their actions are maximised. This leads naturally to our next set of suggestions on matching work to pupils' developing abilities.

While you will find in other chapters in this book many additional suggestions intended to promote the quality of teaching and learning, we hope that those in Chapter 2 are a useful collection of the main recommendations we have to offer in this area.

9

Planning and preparation

According to OFSTED inspection findings, 'The most important direct influence on how well pupils make progress is the teaching they receive. The effectiveness of teaching depends on a number of factors, notably: teacher's knowledge of the subject material and of how it is learned; their expectations of how much pupils can do and learn; and the success of the methods they use in motivating pupils and promoting learning' (OFSTED, 1996). The planning and preparation of lessons is essential to assist in this success.

1   **Make sure that each lesson is part of a structured course**. Each department needs to plan structured schemes of work that fit into the demands of the National Curriculum. These schemes of work also need to reflect the policy decisions made by both the school and the department. If the department is working within its own clearly defined structures, staff and the pupils alike will have confidence in the outcomes.

2   **Match activities to the age and ability of the pupils**. Teachers with a sound knowledge of their subject are able to devise work that is differentiated to match the needs of the pupils in any given class. Differentiation can take a variety of forms. It can be achieved by differentiating the task, the objective, the learning style, the support, and the resource. Teachers' responses will also differ to reflect what the pupil has achieved.

3   **Have clear aims**. It is not enough for the department to have clear aims, each scheme of work should have a clear aim relating to the outcomes expected. This should be true of every lesson within any scheme. If the teacher knows exactly what outcomes are expected, this can then be communicated to the pupils.

4   **Know what the learning objectives are.** If you are clear about what you are trying to achieve, you will communicate this to the pupils. When pupils know what is expected, they will be more likely to achieve those objectives. Use assessment to inform planning for future objectives.

5   **Use a variety of resources.** Make the lesson as interesting as you can. Avoid getting in a rut and using techniques that you know will work. 'Chalk and talk' may work in some situations but is a boring technique if repeated endlessly. Extend your range of teaching styles. Don't be afraid to experiment. You might find that you enjoy it, and the pupils will certainly benefit.

6   **Link aspects of the lesson to the whole curriculum.** As often as you can, make links with other areas of the school curriculum. Pupils find it easy to compartmentalise. Teachers will often hear pupils mutter that what they are discussing in English is really History, or that issues raised in RE they had already discussed in PSE. Pupils often find it hard to have broad perspectives and break down subject-specific barriers.

7   **Link learning to the departmental policies.** Although teachers are bound by the demands of the National Curriculum this does not mean that you cannot adapt that curriculum to reflect ideals that the department or school has devised.

8   **Record the achievement and development of pupils.** Build into the planning of schemes of work a variety of strategies for recording achievement. These benchmarks can be used to assess progress and development.

9   **Lesson planning should reflect a broad and balanced curriculum.** Careful planning avoids falling into the easy trap of placing too much emphasis on an aspect of the curriculum that you enjoy at the expense of the less attractive elements. Planning ensures balance.

10   **Build in progression.** It is easier to build in progression at the planning stage. Carefully structured modules or schemes will have a clear purpose and follow-up processes planned into their design.

10

Learning and teaching strategies

The purpose of teaching is to promote the learning of pupils. Pupils' progress depends on many things and promoting learning depends a great deal on our expectations. We need to have high expectations and challenge pupils in their learning. Teachers need to involve pupils in their own learning. If pupils are merely passive receivers of information they are less likely to be stretched and enthusiastic. Just as staff have to feel ownership of the school planning so pupils need to feel ownership of their learning experiences.

1 **Have high expectations**. Having high expectations pushes pupils to extend themselves. If you do not expect enough the pace of a lesson suffers and pupils can lose motivation. Pupils enjoy being stretched as they can then have pride in their achievement.

2 **Communicate your expectations.** It is easy to write expectations into lesson plans and schemes of work. But it is also easy to forget to tell the pupils, clearly, what you expect of them. When they know where they stand they know what to do.

3 **Build on pupils' own experience**. It is a good idea to start from where the pupils are, and extend ideas from that point. Use what they know or have experienced. This will encourage an identification and empathy and assist understanding of new knowledge.

4 **Use pupils' ideas.** If pupils are interested and involved in their lessons, they will be full of ideas. Pupils will ask questions and offer suggestions. Use them. It makes them feel valued but it also helps to link the new knowledge to their experience. Don't be afraid to leave the planned lesson to explore avenues that have inspired the pupils.

5   **Encourage pupils to predict consequences.** Encouraging pupils to predict the outcomes of their actions and ideas is a valuable tool in the learning process. It helps logical thinking and the use of evidence. They also enjoy the involvement and ownership of their work.

6   **Involve pupils in the evaluation process.** Pupils respond well if they are involved in evaluating their own and each other's work. Involvement is more valuable than pupils simply handing in a piece of work to be marked. If pupils know the criteria for assessment of any particular piece, with practice and guidance, they are quite capable of making accurate judgements on their own levels of performance. This is an excellent learning strategy.

7   **Engage the pupils' attention.** In every lesson it is important to try to engage the attention of all pupils. This is done by varying teaching styles and the use of resources. If all lessons are conducted in the same way pupils quickly become bored and lose motivation. Active learning styles tend to involve all pupils, so spend time devising activities to promote learning and build on their knowledge.

8   **Maintain pupils' involvement.** Having engaged pupils' attention it is important to maintain it. This can be done by having a variety of activities. Using different methods recognises the fact that pupils have varied learning styles and respond in individual ways to tasks. The pace of the lesson should also be varied with some short tasks and others needing longer periods of concentration.

9   **Make effective transitions**. When a lesson involves several different activities or learning steps make sure that these are effective. Pupils need to be able to make connections.

10   **Bring each lesson to a satisfactory conclusion.** Keep a careful eye on the timing of the lessons; this avoids being caught out at the wrong moment or before an activity has reached a satisfactory point to close, otherwise it can leave pupils confused and frustrated.

11

Using IT in the classroom

Pupils learn best when they are using IT themselves rather than just hearing about it. Hands-on classroom work, with support from you, is an essential part of their learning experience. The following suggestions may help you – and your pupils – to get best value from such sessions.

1   **Think about your reasons for using IT in any particular context.** Work out what the intended learning outcomes are, and how they depend on IT being used in the classroom. Tell your pupils what the purpose of using IT is on each occasion you use it.

2   **Don't depend on everything being there and working.** Whether you are · going to use IT yourself to demonstrate something, or get pupils using it to learn something, much depends on everything being in working order. Try to arrange to check the kit before your session.

3   **Make sure that the pupils can see when you demonstrate something.** If they all have networked computers, see if you can relay demonstrations to each workstation. Otherwise, make sure that you are only demonstrating to a small number of pupils at a time, and that they can see exactly what you do at each step.

4   **Put instructions and commands down clearly in handout materials.** It is easier for pupils to work through a numbered sequence of operations, with each instruction short and sharp. It helps a lot when pupils have problems if they can tell you exactly which step is causing them difficulty.

5   **Build in feedback for pupils.** When they are going through an extended sequence of operations, identify stages where they can get positive confirmation that everything is correct up to the stage they have reached. One of the virtues of using IT is that it provides privacy for feedback. This is valuable both to the most able students and those with special educational needs.

6   **Make handouts visual.** Build in from time to time pictures of what pupils' screens should look like at key stages. Programs for printing screen dumps are useful here, allowing you to cut and paste such images into your handout materials.

7   **Identify the stumbling points.** Even with the best prepared handouts and materials, there are usually points when some pupils encounter problems you hadn't thought of. Keep a note of these problems, and adjust your instructions and handout materials to minimise the likelihood of them occurring on future occasions.

8   **Where possible, get pupils learning by doing, at their own pace.** This allows you to walk around acting as troubleshooter and helper. Make sure that your help is equally accessible to pupils in all parts of the room. Have a system whereby pupils needing your help signal you so that you can treat them in order of them alerting you, rather than just the noisiest first.

9   **Make sure that pupils have the chance to consolidate what they have done towards the end of each session.** It is only too easy for pupils to find themselves being rushed to close things down when the session is coming to an end, without them having the chance to make sense of exactly how far they have got, and what remains to be done on the next occasion.

10 **Try to ensure that everyone has a fair crack at the whip.** Where computers are shared, it's easy for some pupils to monopolise the equipment. Think about how you pair or group pupils and consider structuring the sessions so the person with hands on the keyboard changes at intervals.

12

Improving classroom organisation and management

Management of pupils in the class needs to be looked at in terms of the extent to which any particular form of organisation allows the teacher to interact positively and economically with pupils. Inspectors tend to look at what pupils are doing and why, and how long they have to do it. In other words, it is necessary to organise time, resources and activities in order to maximise learning.

1   **Have clear indications that the classroom is a learning environment.** Make sure that the room is tidy. Any litter carelessly dropped in the previous lesson should be cleared away by those pupils before they leave. Start each lesson freshly; there should be no evidence left over from a previous lesson. This provides a positive, new start to each lesson.

2   **Know in advance the organisational structure of the lesson.** Ask yourself if the objectives are best achieved by individual work, pupils working in pairs or small groups, or all pupils working together as a whole class, and prepare accordingly.

3   **Make sure the physical layout of the room is appropriate**. Once you have decided on the most suitable organisational structure for any particular lesson organise the seating and layout in the best possible manner. This is particularly important if you wish pupils to work in groups. Movement in a classroom, especially once the lesson has started, can be disruptive and needs to be managed.

4   **Manage the arrival and departure of pupils**. Have procedures for the start and finish of lessons. Each member of staff will have their own routines. Devise strategies that suit your teaching styles.

5   **Help pupils to know what behaviour is expected.** Just as pupils develop a routine from strategies at the start and finish of lessons, so they need to know what is expected in terms of behaviour. New pupils will try to push the boundaries. It is important for you (and them) to know what those boundaries are.

6   **Display pupils' work.** Pupils feel valued and motivated if their work is displayed. It also sends messages to other pupils as to the standards you expect. It creates a colourful and work-centred environment. But displays need changing constantly for interest, they should not be allowed to get shabby as this gives an impression of lack of care.

7   **Have as many kinds of display material as possible.** Good display material creates a good working environment. It helps stimulate and motivate the pupils. Keep it as fresh and topical as possible. It will need updating as dog-eared displays are worse than none at all.

8   **Maintain a working atmosphere.** This does not automatically imply a silent mass of working bodies. Groupwork is just as productive and often more stimulating, especially if pupils are involved in their task. Productive noise is often more rewarding than enforced silence.

9   **Respond to unexpected or inappropriate behaviour.** Make sure that you respond immediately to any behaviour that you find unacceptable in your lesson. For some pupils a quick glance is enough. Others may need to be asked to leave the room to calm or diffuse the situation. Inappropriate behaviour that distracts others should be dealt with firmly. All pupils should have the right to work undisturbed.

10   **Make sure resources are accessible to all pupils.** Organise the room so that all pupils know where the appropriate resources are, and that these are easily accessible. Once pupils know where things are they can be made responsible for accessing what they need with minimum disruption to the learning of others.

13

Managing relationships

Managing relationships with pupils in the classroom is as important as managing relations with colleagues. A good working environment in the classroom depends on the rapport developed between the pupils and their teacher. Here we offer some tips to foster rewarding and productive relationships. Learning is far more likely to flourish where a relationship is based on mutual trust and respect rather than fear and dominance.

1   **Respect your pupils.** Treat each pupil as an individual, even if you work with very large numbers and find it difficult to distinguish between them. Demonstrate that you genuinely care about their progress. Don't expect respect as a matter of course. Earn respect in the way that you behave towards pupils.

2   **Be genuine.** Pupils are often quicker than adults at sensing when you are putting on a front. They also respond quickly if they think you are genuine and not trying to 'con' them in some way. Pupils respond to people they respect, so it is worth taking time to get to know them and don't pretend to have an understanding of them that you can't support.

3   **Try to establish a rapport with the pupils.** This stems from trying to show pupils that you understand and value their perspectives. Show sympathy when a pupil has a bad cold, or when you know that the school lost at football. The development of a positive climate depends on these types of interchanges.

4   **Act as a good example**. Be aware of the influence your behaviour has on others. Provide a role-model that they can respect. You must practise what you preach; if you are seen to say one thing and do another, it will damage your credibility. If you advocate honesty and are seen to lie to pupils your credibility will soon suffer.

5   **Set your standards.** This follows from acting as an example. Set out the standards of behaviour you expect and carry them out yourself. It is no use expecting pupils to toe the line (for example about leaving the class-room tidy) if you are not prepared to set your own example.

6   **Be civilised**. Be as polite to pupils as you expect them to be to you, even if your expectations are disappointed. Basic courtesies must originate with the teacher. Pupils will behave in class following your example.

7   **Have a sense of humour.** Make a joke at your own expense on occasions. Share with pupils some amusement they see in a situation. It will show your more human side and give you some common ground with your pupils.

8   **Avoid sarcasm.** This form of exchange achieves little except relieving the teacher's feelings. It can reduce people to tears if used to withering effect. Sarcasm might be effective or amusing at the time, but it can damage your relationship with that pupil forever.

9   **Listen to each other.** If you listen to someone, it shows that you respect their contribution. Foster an atmosphere in your classroom where the pupils not only listen to you but listen to and value each other. Build in activities with pairs where pupils take turns to speak or to be silent and listen for minutes at a time. This can help them to get used to the idea of active listening.

10 **Be consistent.** Try to treat all pupils in the same way. Avoid favouritism. Pupils are acutely aware when they think things are not fair. Pupils dislike it when they feel that different people get different treatment.

14

Using a variety of approaches and materials

Using a variety of approaches and materials helps to keep pupils challenged and interested. This enables learning to progress as much as possible in the time available. Often teachers overuse a favoured method as they feel secure and think they know the outcomes. However, this can be counter-productive. Pupils get bored by the same approach each lesson and often do not achieve what was expected if a teacher fails to vary methods appropriately. Approaches can include some of the following techniques. One or more technique can be used in a lesson. But techniques should certainly be varied over time.

1   **Start your session with some form of exposition.** At the beginning of a scheme of work or when introducing a new idea it is helpful to spend some time setting out ideas, information and objectives. This allows pupils to know where they are going and why.

2   **Explain facts and ideas.** Spend time either as a whole class or when the need arises to explain things that pupils don't understand. Questions will often highlight gaps of understanding. Use this opportunity to explain to everyone in the class when necessary.

3   **Demonstrate appropriate techniques that you want pupils to try out for themselves.** This is especially relevant in practical subjects. Pupils need to see a demonstration to understand an idea and they often need to see before they have confidence to try that activity themselves.

4   **Organise discussion sessions**. Class discussions and group discussions are an excellent way to encourage pupils to express themselves orally. Discussion helps promote understanding when pupils verbalise ideas. Discussions can also be valuable in helping pupils to value each other's contributions as well as those of the teachers.

5   **Devise practical exercises**. Many subjects need practical work to enable the pupils to progress, and learning-by-doing is recognised to be extremely valuable. In many subjects, unless the pupils engage in the activity, little learning will take place. Devise as many practical activities as possible for the pupils to take part in individually, in pairs or in small groups. Pupils enjoy the involvement and are motivated to achieve.

6   **Organise investigation activities**. Investigation work encourages pupils to apply their existing learning in new contexts. However, it is necessary to focus this work properly. Make sure also that work is sufficiently demanding for the age and ability of the pupils.

7   **Allow pupils to work alone when necessary.** There are times when silence must be insisted on or where a quiet part of the school needs to be made available. Pupils do need to have that space to concentrate; this allows them to gather their thoughts and reflect on what they are doing.

8   **Pupils can work in pairs.** Working in pairs is a very valuable method of teaching. Some pupils feel intimidated by group activities or whole class discussions. Working with one other person means that both participants have a chance to help each other and extend their ideas and understanding. Sometimes it is helpful to pair pupils of equal ability, but at other times a more able pupil can support the learning of a weaker one.

9   **Organise small group activities.** This type of organisation is useful when you wish discussion to take place about different aspects of a piece of work. If each group has to discuss one aspect of a project and report back it encourages pupils to take responsibility. Pupils are then responsible not only for their group's learning but for communicating that learning to the rest of the class.

10   **Set homework.** Homework is a valuable way of extending work done in the classroom. It is also a way of encouraging pupils' responsibility for their own learning.

15

Fostering pupil involvement and motivation

The National Curriculum requires that pupils learn to work independently. These skills need to be taught. To achieve this the content and resources of lessons need to be carefully chosen. As well as varying the approaches and materials used in lessons pupils need to be supported by clear outlines on the purpose and on the avenues for enquiry. If pupils are involved in their own work learning will take place. They will be motivated to extend their knowledge and work independently.

1   **All pupils should participate fully in the activity set.** If pupils are not participating fully it means they are not involved. Make sure that the activity matches the age and ability of the pupils. If it is not demanding enough pupils will be bored and not fully involved. Similarly, if activities are too difficult pupils will switch off and twiddle their thumbs – or be disruptive.

2   **Pupils need to discuss in class.** Make opportunities for pupil discussions either in pairs or groups. This will help individuals to feel involved in the learning process. If pupils are discussing the topic of the lesson then they are involved.

3   **Make sure that pupils know what is expected of them.** Make any instructions clear and let them know what resources are available, what the timescale is and why they are doing a particular task. If pupils feel uncertain as to expectations they will feel insecure about tackling the exercises set. If they feel insecure they cannot be involved.

4   **Ask someone to explain the task set.** Asking a pupil to explain what they understand the task to involve is a means of making sure that they have understood. It is a way of checking that your instructions or explanations have been clear. It is also a way of assessing the involvement and attention of the class.

5   **Give praise and encouragement.** Make sure that you give praise to pupils whenever possible. We all like to be noticed and valued. Praise encourages and motivates pupils and gives them confidence to improve and extend themselves.

6   **Involve pupils in identifying their own learning outcomes.** Wherever possible involve pupils in their learning. Help pupils to set their own targets. This encourages self-awareness and realistic expectations which will lead to success. Success is a great motivator.

7   **Let pupils have a choice of task.** Where possible devise a range of tasks that will fulfil the aims and objectives of the lesson. Different pupils have different learning styles. Give them a chance to choose their preferred style.

8   **Give as many opportunities as possible for pupils to be responsible for their own learning.** To encourage independent learning try to set up situations where pupils can take responsibility for decisions. Give pupils the options rather than telling them the solutions.

9   **Be flexible.** Avoid being too restricted by the schemes of work. Have a framework for a lesson but be prepared to alter the lesson plan if things do not go as well as expected. Allow time and space in any programme of work to explore avenues that the pupils find interesting, even if they are not written into the programme.

10   **Make IT available in as many lessons as possible.** IT is a valuable option for all pupils. It is of particular value to the least able and to the most able. It is a means of giving them the privacy that they need to develop their own learning. Make the learning outcomes clear so that pupils don't simply play on the computers.

16

Matching the work to pupils' developing ability

Mixed ability teaching requires considerable teacher skill to stretch the most able in the group while at the same time catering for the needs of the least able. There can also be a danger, when groups are set, that the teacher assumes a greater degree of homogeneity than there is. Whatever systems are adopted in school the issues surrounding differentiation are difficult. Schools need to research and respond to differentiation by developing effective teaching and learning approaches. Some of the following issues, according to OFSTED inspectors, need to be addressed.

1   **Plan different provision for different sets.** Make sure that the planned provision for the different sets matches the range of need in that set. This applies also to mixed ability sets. It is useful to recognise that there are a number of methods of differentiation, from varying the tasks and resources to varying the range and type of support and feedback given to pupils.

2   **Challenge pupils appropriately.** Make sure that the tasks set are designed to challenge all pupils. Boredom can lead to disruptive behaviour as easily as pitching a lesson at the wrong level, which in turn can lead to anarchy. This can often be avoided by having open-ended tasks to enable pupils to respond at a range of levels.

3   **Use evidence when placing pupils in sets for given subjects.** Don't assume a uniformity of attainment. Just because a child is in a top set for maths, it does not necessarily follow that the same pupil should be in that set across the board.

4   **Make sure pupils can move sets.** Avoid rigid setting. Enable pupils to move easily between sets if their progress shows that this is appropriate. This should be organised so that they will not lose continuity or progress. It helps to motivate pupils if they feel they can progress rather than feeling they are stuck in a rut whatever they do.

5   **Give equal importance to planning work for all sets.** Avoid concentrating on the high-flying groups in terms of planning and resources. It may be tempting in a time of scarce resources and league tables, but this really isn't a fair or viable option. All resources should be appropriately targeted, especially concerning the reading levels of written materials.

6   **Use funding arrangements to good effect.** Make the best use of the way funding is allocated to direct resources into materials for pupils with special needs. Funding is available and can help with the raising of standards of achievement for such pupils.

7   **Regularly review the effectiveness of setting arrangements.** Don't just set pupils at the beginning of the year and think that is the end of that job. Regular assessment and department meetings will ensure that the pupil is in the right setting arrangement.

8   **Where there are pupils with special needs, develop systems in accordance with the Code of Practice.** This code sets out guidelines for monitoring, reviewing and evaluating procedures in relation to pupils with special needs. Pupils with special needs should also be encouraged to be involved and to take responsibility for their learning. Independence seems to be the key word at every stage and every level.

9   **Use published schemes selectively.** Published schemes of work often appear to be an easy option; but they need to be used selectively to make sure that progress is promoted at all times rather than impeded.

10   **Use as many open questions as possible.** Both oral and written questions benefit from being phrased in an open style. This type of questioning allows pupils to respond at length and in depth, according to their abilities.

Chapter 3 Assessment And Evaluation

Assessment and evaluation are probably the focus of the sharpest end of school improvement. Assessment is in many ways the most public and tangible source of evidence not only of the performance of pupils, but also of the standard of any school. In this chapter, we try to offer practical, but uncompromising, suggestions to help you make assessment and evaluation processes meet the highest quality standards.

We start by looking at the very purposes that assessment should be serving. Our suggestions here take the form of completions of the phrase 'Assessment should...'. While we don't pretend for a moment that it is easy to adjust assessment design and implementation to meet all 10 of these 'shoulds' at once, we strongly recommend that the directions for the improvement of assessment should firmly underpin planning and development. We look next at how best to move from principles to practice and then continue with 20, rather than 10, suggestions on the theme of 'Managing assessment'.

Having now provided recommendations about the ethos of assessment, and about the practical steps that may be taken to achieve this, we continue the chapter with some suggestions about how assessment can be planned. It is important to have a firm strategy for something as crucial as the assessment dimension of teaching and learning, and such a strategy can play a vital role in the overall context of school improvement.

We next move back to thinking about effective learning, and in the context of this chapter, about how this is inextricably connected to assessment. Each and every assignment pupils undertake provides an opportunity for them to get feedback on their performance. There is the danger that when the pressure is on teachers, providing pupils with such feedback may not get as much attention and time as it needs. We therefore offer 20 suggestions on 'Using feedback to enhance learning', in ways not simply aiming to ensure that feedback is effective, but that it can be given efficiently and appropriately.

We end this chapter with suggestions about ways that pupils can be more closely involved in their own assessment. The particular benefits of involving pupils in something as important as their own assessment include them becoming much better acquainted with understanding assessment criteria and how the processes operate, and their learning is deepened and enriched at the same time.

17

Devising clear approaches and purposes for assessment

Clear Statements of Principles for pupil assessment are essential. These should be drawn up in consultation with all staff and departments and agreed by all. These principles can then be incorporated in all departmental and teaching planning. Statements should be broad enough to allow for variations of approach in departments. The following principles can provide a good basis for effective approaches to assessment.

Assessment should...

1   **Be manageable.** Any assessment procedure should be make teaching and learning more effective. If it is too cumbersome or unwieldy, with too much paperwork, it can hinder pupil improvement as the teacher's energy is spent in chasing grades rather than teaching.

2   **Promote learning**. The purpose of all comments and records should be as part of the learning process, so that individual pupil and group progress can be tracked, and problems identified and dealt with. If the records themselves become the object of the exercise and are not used constructively, they are of little value.

3   **Be appropriate.** Assessment will only be valid if the task set matches the specified learning outcomes and the needs of the individual pupils. All too often we assess what is easy to assess rather than what we really want to assess.

4   **Involve pupils.** Pupils need to feel involved in assessment if they are to have some ownership of the process. They need to understand the criteria by which they are being assessed, ideally with opportunities to really get to grips with them by asking lots of questions and rehearsing in trial tasks. This helps them to understand what they are supposed to be doing and encourages responsibility and independent learning.

5   **Motivate pupils.** Students can be motivated by encouragement, praise, clear and prompt feedback about how to improve the quality of their work and guidance about specific actions they need to take to remedy errors. Frequently assessment can demotivate pupils, because it concentrates largely or entirely on their faults and errors, giving little information about remediation of errors and correction of deficiencies.

6   **Reward effort.** This is an integral part of motivation. Positive feedback that helps pupils to understand fully what they have done well, and why it is considered to be good, will help to encourage pupils to keep on working well. Positive feedback is equally important for pupils of all ability levels.

7   **Be understood by all.** Everyone involved needs to understand the criteria that have been used and the way that the results have been described. Numbers on their own are often meaningless unless a frame of reference is provided. Pupils and teachers need to understand the marks recording system fully so they can make sense of the information this provides.

8   **Ensure consistency.** Staff and pupils must be reassured that assessment is being carried out in a way that treats all pupils equally, so that everyone has an equivalent if not identical experience of the process.

9   **Be integral to curriculum design.** Assessment should not be a bolt-on afterthought to the curriculum. All curriculum areas need to plan assessment methods and strategies into their curriculum planning. Departments need to adapt the general school principles to fit into the demands of their subject. Each scheme of work needs to have specific criteria based on the general principles agreed by the school.

10   **Help parents be aware of children's progress.** An important part of the function of keeping records is to inform parents regarding the progress of their child. This will help parents to enter into a partnership in the learning process. It will further assist the pupil in setting realistic targets.

18

From principles to practice

Having agreed on the principles governing the school's assessment and recording policy, there needs to be a development plan. This should be designed to turn your principles into workable practice. Development plans for assessing all areas of the curriculum need to include some of the following.

1 **Include targets in any plan.** These will start from the baseline achievements that you have recorded and indicate how these are likely to improve within a set period.

2 **Devise departmental action plans to implement these targets.** Taking into account local circumstances, each department will need to consider what strategies for assessment they plan to carry out. These should be challenging but achievable.

3 **Decide next what evidence is needed.** This will need to be done within each department so that teachers can assess pupils' progress. Evidence thus achieved can then inform future planning as part of a quality loop.

4 **Limit the number of proposed performance indicators.** These should be few in number, measurable and clearly expressed. Often teams are highly ambitious in the range and scope of improvements they plan to make, or so vague in their plans it is difficult to see whether they have been successful.

5 **Performance indicators should be central to the issue of assessment.** Teams should be asking themselves the questions: 'What evidence do we need in order to demonstrate improved performance?' and 'How can we go about getting evidence in ways that give us the data we really want in a meaningful form?'

6   **Have a balance of the three Qs.** Have a balance of performance indicators that are Quantifiable, Qualitative and Quantitative. These can be used to feed into your overall strategy for improvement.

7   **Build deadlines into your assessment programme.** Without deadlines, it is all too easy to make ambitious plans that can be pushed further and further into the future.

8   **Build into your strategies planning for the future**. All assessment should provide evidence for further improvement or planning. Data that does not help you do this is, for the most part, not really worth the effort of collecting.

9   **Devise a strategy for assessment that ensures pupils experience all kinds of assessment**. Different methods will be needed to assess the various aspects of the curriculum. Different kinds of skill need a number of methods of assessment. All forms of assessment discriminate against some of your pupils, so arrange that they experience a mixed diet of methods.

10 **Plan an assessment strategy that is cost-effective.** Be realistic in terms of the time spent on any one form of assessment. Is it value for money? If teachers are overburdened and exhausted, question whether the result of that form of assessment could be achieved by an alternative method.

19

Managing assessment

Since it is impossible and undesirable to assess everything at once, it is essential to decide on criteria for assessment. Everyone would like to be able to assess less and be more efficient in their marking. The art of assessment is to find the best ways to assess what you really want to assess at the right time, so that assessment is valid, reliable, manageable and fit for purpose. These tips aim to help you do it better.

1   **Assess less, better.** Look for ways to ensure that you can maintain the rigour of assessment and give pupils lots of feedback, without making life impossible for yourself. Query whether you are setting too many repetitive tasks that test the same things again and again.

2   **Consider ways of speeding up your assessment.** You could, perhaps, use assignment return sheets or statement banks when you find yourself writing the same comments repeatedly or use self or peer grading where correct answers are available to check against. This makes sense for all concerned. Teachers can get so overwhelmed by the processes of assessment that the product can get submerged.

3   **Use the 'best fit' approach.** The art of assessment is to check that you are really clear about the purposes, the validity, the reliability and the manageability of assessment approaches. Choosing the right methods, who does the assessment and its timing, is also crucial. This will help you devise a 'fit for purpose' strategy, since these factors are all interdependent.

4   **Consider why you are assessing.** Reasons might include to classify pupil achievement, guide subject choice, motivate pupils, provide formative feedback, provide summative grades, estimate individual progress and so on. The purpose of assessment will help you make decisions about how and what you require pupils to do.

5　**Think about what you are assessing.** Are you, for example, assessing the product or the process by which it is created. Are you assessing the pupil's ability to do something or, as is often the case, whether the pupil can write about doing it.

6　**Use a wide range of techniques for assessment.** Which is the best product to evaluate what you are aiming to assess? Consider whether it could be an essay, a multiple-choice test, short answer questions, oral presentations, poster displays, exhibitions, aesthetic products such as poems or plays, artefacts such as garments or sculptures, problem sheets, lab reports, mind maps, portfolios, annotated bibliographies.

7　**Think about the right type of assessment for the learning outcomes**. The type of assessment task that you choose will be dependent on what you are assessing. You should aim to offer a wide range of assessment styles in the same way as you offer a wide range of learning styles.

8　**Think about who is best placed to assess**. This could be the teacher, when specific expertise and knowledge is needed to make judgements; peers when it is a matter of group process or when the criteria have been made sufficiently explicit to enable pupils to make as equally valid judgements as the teacher; externals, such as employers or parents where a different perspective is valued; or individual pupils themselves where it is a matter of reflection or personal development.

9　**Consider when assessment should take place.** Sometimes this will be at the end of a period of learning. At other times, continuous assessment is most appropriate. Where assessment is end-point, there is often little need to put much energy into providing detailed feedback. If it is mid-point, it is not always necessary to provide summative marks.

10　**Change your routines to meet your current assessment needs.** It is all too easy to keep using the same assessment methods and strategies when these no longer serve the purpose for which they were originally designed. Beware also of simply adding to your burden by bringing in new methods without displacing the old ones.

11　**Use classroom management techniques that encourage self-sufficiency.** Involve pupils in checking their own work against model answers or tick sheets. Make good use of computer-assisted learning (CAL) packages where these exist, so pupils can get feedback on computerised tests to help them get the measure of their own performance. Wherever possible adopt styles of assessment that encourage independent learning and self-sufficiency.

12 **Try some team teaching and assessment**. It can be difficult to teach and assess pupils' achievements at the same time. Look for ways in which you can use colleagues to support you so that in-class assessment can take place in parallel to teaching. It is also useful to have a second opinion on your pupils' achievements, so you can work towards avoiding bias.

13 **Think about inter-tutor reliability.** Can you be sure that two or more tutors will be giving the same grade to a given piece of work? To help reliability you need all or both to have a clear understanding of the criteria and what they really mean in practice. A marking protocol can be helpful, giving clear descriptions of what performances would look like for each of the criteria in each of the assessment grades.

14 **Think too about intra-tutor reliability**. Would you reliably give the same mark to the same piece of work at different times? Does the mark you give depend on the order in which you have marked it? Do you (like most people) tend to give most marks around the average when you are tired? You need to keep looking back to the criteria and occasionally cross-checking your own marks.

15 **Swap classes for assessment.** This is another way to take a fresh look at the work of pupils that you are familiar with. Your colleague may be able to make judgements about achievement that are not coloured by pupils' behaviour and demeanour in class.

16 **Set achievable targets**. This applies both to yourself and to the pupils. Avoid giving pupils too many tasks to undertake which puts pressure on you and on them. Your aim should be for high-quality assessment, rather than high-quantity assessment.

17 **Select materials to assess.** Annotated folders of selected pieces of work are much more valuable than a mass of undifferentiated materials. Asking pupils to annotate their work to demonstrate their learning can be valuable too.

18 **Check whether your assessment methods are fair.** Has each pupil been given ample opportunities to demonstrate a range of activities on which to base these records, rather than a single 'sudden death' task?

19 **Check whether you are assessing appropriately**. Quantity of work should not be the only criteria. It is useful to look for variety, excellence and progression.

20   **Record information appropriately.** A lot of energy can be spent in chasing pieces of work that have been lost or trying to locate mark lists that have been misplaced. Work out a system (electronic or otherwise) to help you keep track of assessment data and be scrupulous in maintaining it.

20

Using feedback to enhance learning

Providing good feedback for pupils is crucial in helping them know how they are doing and can be a major contributor to individual and cohort improvement. It takes time and energy to do well, but this is a worthwhile investment in terms of learning pay-off.

1 **Give good feedback.** Best practice assessment comprises description, evaluation and remediation. Feedback should contain all of these elements if it is to help pupils improve. Pupils need to recognise what you are saying relates to their own work, get an idea of how well they are doing, and know what to do next.

2 **Be sensitive in your feedback.** Pupils can become demotivated if they feel that they are being attacked personally by your critique. Concentrate on the work itself rather than the person and try to avoid dismissive language that leaves no room for improvement.

3 **Encourage pupils to participate in the assessment and recording process.** Involving pupils raises standards by fostering self-determination and can be a great motivator. Pupils often like to be able to see their marks improving over a period of time, and don't like to fall behind against their own 'personal best' scores.

4 **Assessment should identify both strengths and weaknesses.** Tell them what is right with what they have done as well as what is wrong and help them know what they need to do to make it better. Start with the positive – but remember that assessment achieves little if it does not help to identify areas for improvement.

5   **Feedback to pupils should be speedy.** Unless feedback is provided to pupils as swiftly as possible, they tend to lose interest in the work and the chance to make improvements can be lost. It is a dreadful waste of time to write lengthy comments on work that are not read because the original assignment is now history.

6   **Feedback should be constructive.** Frame your comments in ways that help pupils to feel motivated to improve. The identification of weaknesses does not have to mean destructive criticism and constructive ideas of how to improve are an essential part of assessment.

7   **Feedback should motivate, be helpful and encouraging**. Assessment techniques should celebrate achievement as well as motivating further study. Pupils should feel encouraged to progress further even if they have already done reasonably well.

8   **Assessment should assist in meaningful dialogue.** Make time for pupils to look at and think about the comments made on their work. Use feedback to stimulate a meaningful dialogue with the pupils to encourage self-awareness and target-setting for future learning.

9   **Pupils should have a clear understanding of expectations**. Clarify the assessment objectives of each task set and tell the pupils which particular aspect of their work they can expect feedback on in any individual assignment. Avoid giving feedback on too many aspects at once.

10   **Base assessment records on a variety of types of assessed activities.** Records should be based on a variety of evidence, so vary your assessment approaches and avoid using evidence from a single source such as the end-of-term examination.

11   **Use records to provide feedback**. Provide these in appropriate formats so that the different stakeholders (pupils, fellow teachers, moderators and parents) can make sense of them. Complex data in the form of tables and graphs often required by externals can seem mystifying to pupils who are often less interested in how the school as a whole is doing against historical data than in how they are doing themselves compared to their peers at the moment.

12 **Offer dialogue to promote learning.** Show an interest in the work. Give comments that need a response from the pupil. 'Well done' is a general closed comment. Such comments offer no possibility for dialogue.

13 **Respond to meaning, not just surface features**. It is often easier to rush through work marking the surface features such as spelling, grammatical mistakes or calculation errors. This achieves little except a lot of red lines. Respond to what a pupil is trying to achieve as well as what they have achieved.

14 **Use written responses to ask questions.** Show an interest by asking questions. Give your views on the topic and then invite their comments verbally or in writing. Assignments can involve meaningful written dialogue as well as spoken.

15 **Ask for pupils' opinions on your views.** This is particularly good with shy pupils. They can have a private written dialogue with the teacher. The teacher can also set tasks in relation to the work, further possibilities to explore or sections to revise.

16 **Concentrate on one major feature.** Sometimes teachers say a pupil's work is full of mistakes, when often they mean there are one or two mistakes made many times. Don't correct everything. This is unfocused and confusing to the pupil. Identify one or two items for the pupil to focus on.

17 **Help pupils to identify one area to concentrate on for improvement**. As part of an assessment dialogue, help pupils to identify their own areas of focus. They are far more self-aware that we often give them credit for.

18 **Don't respond to everything.** Don't feel the need to make a full written response on all written work to all things every time. This can be demotivating to the pupil and not a valuable use of teacher time. Decide in advance which pieces will be marked for which aspects of learning.

19 **Explain the main area of focus.** Explain to the pupils which area you will be focusing on in any assessment, what you will be looking for and how you will be assessing it.

20 **Provide an audience for work.** All assessment provides a pupil with an audience for their work. Make sure pupils value that audience by your responses to their work. This will be reflected in the quality of work that you in turn receive.

21

Involving pupils in assessment to improve learning

Involving pupils in their own assessments is good practice that helps ensure achievement for all. Involving pupils is a classroom management technique that encourages self-sufficiency. Independence in learning is now a National Curriculum requirement.

1 **As a department identify areas where pupils can be involved.** Most departments can find some areas where it is possible for pupils to be involved in their own and each other's assessment. It helps pupils to have self-determination and it relieves the teacher of some assessment tasks.

2 **Be prepared to let go.** This can be difficult if you are inclined to feel that only the teacher knows what to look for. But careful guidelines to pupils help them take on some of the responsibility.

3 **Start with pupil involvement in descriptive records.** It is easier to start with pupils keeping descriptive records relating to the types of tasks undertaken. In English departments pupils can be asked to keep records of the books read, or in science departments, ask pupils to record experiments they do. When pupils are familiar with recording descriptive tasks, it is easier to progress to evaluation techniques.

4 **Gradually introduce evaluative tasks.** It is not a very large step to add small evaluative tasks. 'Why did you enjoy the book?' 'How did the experiment work?' are simple questions to start the process. If this is done early on, introducing more complex evaluative tasks becomes a natural part of the education process.

5   **Give pupils clear outlines of what you are assessing.** It gives pupils security to know exactly what is expected from them. Having started with basic tasks gradually introduce more complex criteria. Let them know what they are hoping to achieve and what indicators to look for in assessing that achievement.

6   **Get pupils to swap pieces of work and mark each other's.** Pupils enjoy reading their friends' work and quickly take on the responsibility. This is an excellent way of enabling pupils to understand assessment criteria.

7   **Use exemplar material and carry out whole class activities of assessment.** When the piece of work being analysed does not belong to them or their friends it is easier to feel free to comment both encouragingly and constructively.

8   **Ask pupils to set targets.** These should be based on the assessment of any particular piece of work, its merits and its shortcomings. If pupils understand and know the teacher's expectation it is easy to set themselves specific targets.

9   **Discourage general targets.** Encourage pupils to avoid general targets such as 'I must try harder', or 'I must spend more time'. Ask them what they must try harder at or what they must spend time on. Bear in mind the SMART criteria, which suggest that targets should be Specific, Measurable, Achievable, Realistic and Time-constrained.

10   **Make sure pupils assess a range of work.** This will show them what the best in the class are capable of. This develops a self-awareness and a more realistic approach to their own work. It also raises an individual's expectation.

11   **Give pupils responsibility.** In some assessment exercises insist that it is only the pupil involvement that will go on record. This encourages involvement and self-respect.

Chapter 4 Staff Development

Staff development is naturally a fundamental process underpinning the broad picture of school improvement. We start this chapter with two sets of recommendations for consideration when drawing up school policies on staff development. The first set looks at the role of a staff development policy in the context of addressing the provision of guidance, counselling and support for staff. We follow this with suggestions about how such a policy statement may best be researched and devised, starting from where the school is at the time of planning it.

We next move on to some of the practicalities, starting with ways of fostering the staff motivation. However good a staff development policy may be, staff motivation remains a prerequisite if the policy is to be brought to successful fruition.

Mentoring new members of staff can be one of the most important processes to predetermine levels of motivation, and it underpins the ethos of staff development in a school. We offer some practical suggestions on ways in which such mentoring can be implemented.

Action planning is vital for any proposed development, and staff development is no exception to this. We offer some suggestions about how action planning can be linked to staff development planning, particularly including recommendations about widening the membership of those who contribute to action planning in this context.

We next move on to suggestions about strengthening the links between school development policies and staff development processes, and then end this chapter with some points on the differences and overlaps between performance assessment and performance tracking. Staff development is inextricably linked with any school's appraisal system. We cover this area later in Chapter 7.

22

Providing guidance, counselling and training for staff

Staff development is a complex activity that cannot simply be left to happen. It needs to be managed, and in managing staff development the stress should be on continuous improvement. In most schools staff development requires an open, supportive and participative management structure. To enable schools to achieve continual improvement, schools need to consider each of the recommendations set out below.

1   **Develop a clear, shared staff development policy.** This does not need to be elaborate. However, it is beneficial if all staff have been involved in the process of formulating the policy and of prioritising needs. All staff will then feel commitment to the policy document and cooperate in carrying out the principles involved.

2   **Incorporate into the staff development policy a statement of values.** This statement should be about the principles underlying staff development. These principles should be agreed by all staff through some form of consultation process. If the values underpinning the staff development policy in the school are owned by all, their implementation will be more effective.

3   **Draw up a statement of more specific objectives for staff development.** Once a statement of values and principles governing staff development have been agreed, more specific objectives can be determined. These objectives should grow out of the principles already established and can be continually modified in the light of the needs of the staff and the school.

4   **Devise a consultative structure for individual teachers.** This may be in the form of existing appraisal systems. However, since this process, at the moment, is worked on a two-year cycle, extra support and information mechanisms will need to be in place.

5   **Devise a statement outlining the entitlement of support any teacher might expect.** This statement could include what might be expected during an induction year, what is expected after appraisal and what regular INSET provision is available in the school.

6   **Allocate a budget for staff development.** Appraisal should come within this budget in terms of both resources and staff time. The needs and demands originating from appraisal can then be incorporated into this budget.

7   **Indicate how the resource allocation is to be divided.** Decide how much you will spend on individual career development, how much on personal development and how much on curriculum change. This avoids misunderstandings and false hopes, or unrealistic expectations being raised.

8   **Link policy to action**. Make sure the decisions are realistic, achievable and within time constraints. Without these links staff development policies have a way of lying in a cupboard as merely a paper exercise.

9   **Strike a sensible balance between the needs of the individual and the needs of the school.** Individuals need to extend their range, scope and expertise. The school will also feel the need to address broader issues. Where a school has a shared policy these aims can be married.

10 **Ensure there is adequate support for staff.** Any given member of staff will have an appraiser. New members of staff will have a mentor. However, an appraiser and mentor do not have to be the same person. You may find it helpful to split the role of assessor and personal confidant, although both are probably necessary.

23

Devising staff development policies

Every school needs to have a staff development policy statement, which needs to be linked to school development planning. Any staff development policy needs to demonstrate the links between staff and school development. Although staff development appears to be concerned with individual development, with shrinking school budgets it is essential that the needs of the school and the needs of the individual are drawn as closely together as possible. Involving all staff in the process of a school review to link school development and staff development are crucial elements in any school improvement programme.

1   **Conduct a school-based self-review.** This will involve all staff in assessing the needs of the school and enable staff to feel a commitment to school improvement and to their own personal staff development. It helps staff to identify with the school. A starting point can be the same SWOT analysis (Strengths, Weaknesses, Opportunities and Threats) that was conducted when devising the school development plan.

2   **Ask where the school stands now.** Any review needs to ask this question at the outset. It allows strengths to be recognised and weaknesses to be acknowledged. It also involves looking at all the opportunities that exist for improvement as well as discussing any threats there are to the success of the development.

3   **Ask how well the school is performing.** This can be done by looking at such things as exam results, unauthorised absences and the amount of graffiti. Performance indicators chosen for review will vary in each school.

4   **Ask where the school wants to go.** It is useful here to set a few targets that are both achievable and measurable. Once a school has established benchmarks from existing data it is easier to discuss the weaknesses and decide on the most useful staff development programme to raise standards.

5   **Make sure everyone is involved in the process.** If everyone is involved it leads to a feeling of ownership of the policy. Staff are then more likely to cooperate in its implementation.

6   **Make it a continual process.** Just as individual self-appraisal is a continuing process so is a school self-review. School self-review is a continual cyclical process so any policy needs to be flexible.

7   **Emphasise the purpose of staff development.** This is to make people feel valued in their job and to contribute to improved teaching and learning in a school improvement programme.

8   **Show how resources of time are to be allocated**. Any policy needs to set out clear timescales for initiatives and projects.

9   **Write into the policy how the financial resources are to be allocated**. This is part of an open management style. If staff know how and why money is being spent it leads to cooperation and motivation.

10   **Build in evaluation mechanisms.** Having decided on the targets, a school needs to devise performance indicators to measure the degrees of success of the agreed priorities.

24

Fostering motivation of staff

When there is an open consultative management approach in schools staff feel a sense of identification and ownership of the policies of that school. Once that identification is developed, staff feel motivated and valued. The appraisal system has proved an invaluable tool in fostering a positive and active response to staff development and school improvement.

1   **Use appraisal to give positive feedback.** The appraisal process is an ideal situation for the appraiser and appraisee to develop an excellent working relationship. An appraiser should always start with the positive. Everyone feels good if their achievements are recognised.

2   **Recognise and acknowledge the skills of an individual teacher.** Use an appraisal system to increase motivation by recognising the skills of individual teachers. Use these skills as part of your staff development programme. Teachers feel flattered when asked to share their expertise.

3   **Organise peer coaching strategies.** It is one of the highest compliments that you can pay anyone when you ask them to share or demonstrate their expertise with others. Coaching another person offers excellent staff development opportunities for both parties.

4   **Devise a framework for staff to disseminate new knowledge and skills.** Staff who undertake any external INSET should be given the opportunity to share their knowledge with others. This offers the giver high prestige and the receivers an opportunity to gain new skills or knowledge themselves. INSET needs should be coordinated in relation to an individual's appraisal targets.

5   **Use the follow-up interview to develop good relationships.** Both the appraiser and the appraisee benefit from the relationships formed in an appraisal cycle. Appraisees feel valued if they are given time to talk about themselves and their staff development; appraisers also feel valued for being able to give their help and advice.

6   **Provide meaningful feedback.** After any observation teachers want to hear meaningful comments, linked to observable factors in the lesson. It can often seem patronising to offer broad and bland statements. Constructive criticism does not mean destruction.

7   **Acknowledge and celebrate strengths.** So often teachers' jobs are conducted behind closed doors. Appraisal is a formal, and hopefully non-threatening, means of teachers sharing experience.

8   **Collect data from a wide range of people.** This can help to motivate. If information comes only from the observation of teaching skills and not from other aspects of a person's job, then individuals will feel undervalued. If the collection of data is biased, appraisal will then be viewed as too narrow and restrictive.

9   **Appoint a member of staff with responsibility for staff development.** This means that clear lines of communication can be devised. It also means that if the targets from appraisal systems are channelled to the staff development coordinator, coherent policies for staff development can be devised. When this happens, all members of staff feel that their contribution is valued.

10 **Create a climate in school where appraisal is seen as a useful process.** Appraisal should be viewed as a mechanism that helps learning for all. This will happen when staff begin to see results and when resources, however small, are used to meet the identified needs.

25

Mentoring new members of staff

Teachers in their first year of teaching usually flourish if they are given plenty of support. A mentoring system helps new staff to settle into the job, find their feet and develop personally and professionally. Schools with good mentoring systems help new teachers to become productive members of staff early on in their careers and encourage them to stay on and contribute to the school. These tips offer some ideas on how to do it well.

1 **Choose mentors appropriately.** They do best if they are interested in being mentors (not just having the job foisted on them) with plenty of ideas, able and willing to give time to the task, ready to share concerns with other mentors, focused in approach and able to inspire confidence.

2 **Choose mentors of the right calibre.** They should be people who are in a position to influence the leadership of the department or school, senior in some respect to the mentee (but not their direct line manager) and in a position that is secure in status.

3 **Set up a system for mentoring.** There should be direct involvement (or demonstrated commitment) of senior management, who may be able to act as role-models in the scheme, with clear management structures for directing the scheme and an effective monitoring system.

4 **Train your mentees and mentors**. This does not have to be extensive or formal, but should be designed so that all parties know what can reasonably be expected of them.

5 **Value your mentors.** Make sure that the work is part of their agreed commitments and don't expect them just to do it alongside everything else.

6   **Make time for mentoring**. Try to schedule regular times for mentors to talk to mentees and each other. Give your mentors the chance to swap experiences and exchange good ideas about how to do the job well.

7   **Encourage informal 'corridor mentoring'**. The informal support on a day-to-day basis that mentors give can be the most valuable kind. Mentees ought to feel they can share small problems as well as the big issues with their mentees.

8   **Encourage co-mentoring**. Encourage your new teachers to discuss how they are doing with each other. Simply having someone willing to listen to problems is a help. Once mentees have overcome any feeling that they have to cope wonderfully on their own, they can get the most out of using each other as a powerful aid to their learning.

9   **Promote all kinds of mentoring support.** This can include watching the mentee teach, providing encouragement, troubleshooting, helping them deal with different problems, simply being available for a chat, helping mentees feel good about what they have already achieved, 'knowing someone who can' when they can't offer direct help themselves, helping mentees plan their work, cultivating mentees' feelings ('go on – you can do it', 'you're not on your own'), and providing a shoulder to cry on when things go badly.

10   **Monitor the process.** Without setting up an excessively formal structure, ask mentors to keep records of mentoring sessions, not necessarily giving a great deal of detail, but more to provide some kind of structure to the programme.

26

Action planning for development

Devising a school development policy and firmly linking this to staff development helps to ensure that action planning for the future can take place. Using an open management style means that the whole group is involved and that the planning is shared by all. The very process itself is developmental and individuals should be made to feel confident to go on to produce their own action planning.

1   **Focus attention on the aims of education.** Especially focus on the learning and achievement of all pupils. This can be within the broadly defined context of the school and its mission statement. Encourage teachers to be flexible and innovative in their styles and to have the confidence to encourage independent learning in their pupils.

2   **Set out a coordinated approach.** This will need to include curriculum planning, assessment, teaching and management, as well as finance and resources. All departmental policies need to be coordinated within the broader context of school policies, while at the same time allowing freedom for each department to develop their own ideas.

3   **Capture the long-term vision of the school.** This vision will have been articulated during the review stage of the planning and should become second nature to all members of staff. The general ethos of any school should be all-pervading and filter to all aspects of the school's management.

4   **Set short-term manageable goals.** This helps to relieve the stress of change. Individuals will feel more in control of the pace of change and not feel swept away in a tide of innovation.

5   **Give recognition.** All staff feel more confident if their particular innovations and changes are recognised. Try to build in a structure that enables the recognition of achievement of all staff. We tend to recognise achievement in pupils but forget to extend that same encouragement to staff. Recognition gives confidence to continue and develop ideas further.

6   **Involve Governors.** They not only have a responsibility to the school but they usually have a keen interest in its success. Therefore, they offer valuable contributions in determining priorities and assisting in action planning.

7   **Invite outsiders to help and provide advice.** This could be external consultants or the LEA advisers. Any extra help in reviewing and discussion is valuable. Sometimes we are too close to our own institution and don't always view objectively. Teachers are often very good at finding the shortcomings of their school but are often not as good at celebrating its strengths.

8   **Involve parents.** There is a lot of untapped expertise locked up in parents' experiences. Use it as a valuable free resource. Parents will bring a fresh perspective.

9   **Involve the local community and business.** This will mean that the communication process becomes varied and that the school reflects the needs of its particular environment as well as the general needs of the society.

10 **Make sure that the goals and targets are understood by all.** A feeling of co-ownership fostered in the review stage will enable individuals to participate in creating a climate of evaluation. This in turn paves the way for productive INSET.

27

Linking school and staff development policies

School reviews are an essential part in the process of linking school and staff development policies. School reviews should be part of a cyclical process. Review leads to decision, these decisions in turn lead to actions, which in their turn lead to evaluation. Evaluations of success lead to more reviews. In the light of those evaluations priorities for action can be determined and we are eventually led back to another reviewing process.

1   **Establish what is current practice and policy.** This seems to be a useful starting point in any review or audit. Reviews can be in the form of a formal questionnaire or can be through staff development discussion time. It is helpful to seek documentary evidence to support these views. You can also use current records to establish the benchmarks.

2   **Try to find out what really happens.** Often lip service is paid to what people think should happen, which can be far removed from the actuality. Focus on the real – what is really happening. Only then can forward progress be made.

3   **Agree criteria for assessing procedures and practice**. Once you have established what is actually happening in the school by consulting existing records (or compiling new or different ones), it is possible to arrive at some criteria for assessing any procedures you might put in place.

4   **Carry out the procedures.** Apply the criteria and see how successful they are. Follow this with consultation as to the effectiveness of current practice. If they don't work, rethink ways of assessment of success.

5   **Modify and alter practice if necessary.** Avoid feeling that policies and plans are written in tablets of stone. Development planning should be flexible and part of a continuous cycle. If something does not produce the results you intended then modify the plans. Don't be afraid to try new things.

6   **Identify the main conclusions.** There will be a broad consensus regarding the successful changes. It will then be possible to put forward recommendations for development.

7   **Link the conclusions to the staff development programme.** Once a school has conducted a review and decided on the school development priorities these can be linked to staff development This cyclical process of modification and change must be ongoing and continually open to change as the needs of the school develop.

8   **Link school-based targets to individual appraisal targets.** Choose at least one of the agreed school development targets to be incorporated into the staff development programme. The easiest way to do this is through the appraisal system.

9   **Put in place procedures to achieve the targets set.** Having answered the question 'Where do we want to be?', the next question is, 'How do we get there?' This involves action planning. The targets are set for short- and long-term action; now you need procedures to enable people to achieve them.

10   **Devise performance criteria to help assess how you are doing.** 'When you can measure what you are speaking about and express it in numbers, you know something about it.' (Attributed to the physicist Lord Kelvin.)

28

Performance assessment or performance tracking

You cannot tell people to do their best and then hope that their best is good enough. You (and they) have to know how they are doing and where they, and the school, can improve. This is a modified quotation from Carl Sewell's *The Golden Rule of Customer Care*, and is quoted in a performance assessment package devised and used by Armstrong Watson, a firm of accountants. Within this context the pupils are our customers; therefore, the same ideas are both valid and useful. Measurement is a key element of success. Measurement not only provides data and benchmarks, it also encourages positive change. Using these tools a school has evidence of its performance and a base level from which to assess and improve.

1   **Demonstrate the need for change**. Unless you can show that there is such a need it will be difficult to implement change. The school review and audit is a good starting point.

2   **Have a written but flexible plan**. This plan should incorporate realistic goals and targets, wherever possible expressed in numbers. These targets should not be rigid and should be updated as part of the ongoing evaluation process.

3   **Choose numbers that matter.** There is little point in choosing numbers over which you have no control, or that have little perceived relevance. Give these performance indicators names – it helps to concentrate the mind. An example might be the unauthorised absentee ratings, if this is a problem in your school.

4   **Use information from current records**. Not only does this provide you with a benchmark from which to track performance, it reduces the risk of creating record-keeping. In the case of truanting the records are readily available. Other performance indicators might be formulated around parental complaints, the bullying diary, etc.

5   **Consider assessment by those in a position to judge performance.** It would not be impossible to ask students to assess, or score particular courses. A low performance indicator could give early warning of, for example, truancy problems ahead.

6   **Set SMART targets.** In the light of your benchmarks, or historical performance indicators, set SMART targets – Specific, Measurable, Agreed, Realistic and Time-constrained.

7   **Plot performance.** A picture paints a thousand words. By continuous measurement of performance indicators, it is possible to plot the rate of change on a graph, which might include last year's performance and current targets. This provides a very visible means of communicating success.

8   **Keep the process going.** It is easier to start a new initiative than to restart an old one. Regular evaluation meetings, to discuss the performance indicators, will keep the process going.

9   **Modify the development plan**. The evaluation of the movement of the performance indicators will highlight areas where plans need to be modified and, possibly, targets reassessed.

10   **Link training to development plans and modified targets**. Training for the sake of training is a waste of time.

Chapter 5 Developing Skills For School Improvement

In earlier chapters of this book we have made suggestions about the rationale underpinning school improvement, and indicated some of the main factors that need to be addressed when implementing change. In this chapter, we turn our attention to some of the skills and attributes needed by colleagues involved in school improvement.

We start with teamwork. Teamwork doesn't just happen. Behind the operation of any successful team, strategies and practices are in place that help to develop the collaborative working which makes teams function effectively. We suggest some approaches that can help to ensure that staff in a department, or in a whole school, develop the sense of ownership of progress that comes with good teamwork.

We move next to high expectations. These are not achieved in isolation, but in the broad scenario of every process involved in running a department and a school. We offer some suggestions which, when combined together, lead to increased levels of expectation from teachers, and in turn from pupils.

An essential part of learning is 'doing', and in our suggestions on 'Achieving learning for all' we suggest processes for ensuring that staff have the opportunities to develop new skills that will help achieve school improvements.

Next we turn to some of the processes that are useful in building relationships, both with colleagues and with pupils. The better the quality of such relationships, the more that can be achieved collaboratively in terms of school improvement.

'Questioning skills' are a vital part of any good teacher's toolkit. For pupils, the act of answering questions is a strong learning experience, and the better the questions, the deeper the learning. We give some 'do's and don't's on questioning. Closely related to questioning skills are listening skills. At least as many people are 'hard of listening' as are 'hard of hearing', but they don't usually know it! We provide some suggestions about ways of actively developing your listening techniques, which pay dividends not only in your work with pupils, but in your interactions with colleagues.

Our next two sets of suggestions are about feedback – giving it, and receiving it. Sometimes, teachers appear to be more concerned about the giving of feedback, as it is an essential part of their work with pupils. However, it is also important to be skilled at receiving feedback from both colleagues and students, not least because this helps us be better at giving it appropriately.

Recording of information can be a nightmare. It can also take up more time and energy than we've got! We therefore include some suggestions to help make the information that is recorded as useful as possible, and recorded in ways that lend themselves to all of the most important uses of such records.

We end this chapter with some suggestions on negotiation skills. We all know how disastrous things can be when such skills are missing at an important decision-making stage. Negotiation skills are every bit as important in teaching and learning as they are in planning school improvement.

29

Fostering teamwork

Teamwork is important throughout any school organisation. When people work in isolation, they tend to stay behind a closed door, locked in with their pupils. While all teachers are individual and autonomous beings, it is not enough that they simply stay in their classroom and work in splendid isolation. Teamwork allows for a cross-fertilisation of ideas and an expansion of skills. There can be no individual development without teamwork, therefore, school improvement depends critically upon collaboration.

1   **Be mutually supportive.** It is a good idea for all members of a group or department to support and encourage each other. This clearly applies to new teachers who need help and support. But all individuals like to feel part of a team. It gives a sense of belonging.

2   **Agree a departmental statement.** This enables all members of a department to share the same vision about their subject, their aims and their expectations. It develops a collegiate responsibility.

3   **Have regular meetings.** Meetings allow the disparate individuals, especially in a large secondary school, where staff often have to teach a non-specialist subject, to come together and share good practice. Things that have been successful with one member of a department are usually helpful to others. However, the way people behave in groups needs careful management, as some will resist change and can block progress. Team-building activities may be important.

4   **Have departmental standardisation meetings.** This is an excellent staff development technique. It also encourages teamwork when all members of a department come together and share work and expectations, and it is useful to develop a departmental sense of ownership of standards.

5   **Compile benchmarks within a department.** Using existing information from pupils (this applies at all Key Stages) it is possible to compile evidence of where you are in terms of standards. From these benchmarks it is possible to set future targets within your department.

6   **Agree on a marking policy.** This will lead to discussions on expectations and standards. These standards will then need to be agreed by all in the department. Any discussion and debate within a department helps to encourage a shared vision, which is crucial in something as important as assessment procedures.

7   **Use the information gathered.** Data gathered on performance can then be used to inform subsequent work and planning. Departments can judge where they are and where they want to be.

8   **Promote consistency.** By having regular meetings, discussing progress and devising marking policies, teamwork is established which helps to promote consistent approaches within a department. (The same applies for wider management issues.) Consistency usually means that pupils have clear guidelines and are therefore able to achieve higher standards.

9   **Involve all the department in the decision-making processes.** Even the teachers who have just arrived or those who only teach a few lessons of the subject can offer valuable ideas. They also need to feel ownership of any policies that they are expected to follow.

10   **Develop participatory leadership.** Rotating responsibilities for certain aspects of work within the department means that each member of a department has a chance for further individual development. A wide range of experience is clearly developmental. It is also developmental for middle management to delegate responsibilities and prioritise their own actions.

30

Encouraging high expectations

In order to encourage high expectations from pupils, a good starting point within any given department is to promote subject-specific staff development. When people are confident in handling their material they will then be confident to insist on higher standards from their pupils. OFSTED in the *Subjects and Standards* publication advises regular subject-specific staff development.

1   **Have a confident grasp of your subject.** If you feel confident you will pass that confidence on to the pupils. This will encourage pupils to have high expectations of themselves knowing they will receive the support and help from the teacher.

2   **Be aware of different methods of teaching**. A variety of methods helps to ensure that you cater for all learning styles. This enables all pupils to achieve. It also stops disruptive behaviour that can arise when pupils are not being stretched. Using a variety of methods stops boredom creeping in – for both the pupil and the teacher!

3   **Make your subject interesting.** Try to stimulate pupils' imagination and ideas as much as possible. Devise exercises that will involve the pupils and encourage independence in their learning. This will stretch pupils to achieve their maximum.

4   **Love your subject.** If you communicate a love of your subject to the pupils they cannot help but respond – enthusiasm is catching. Your enthusiasm communicates itself to the pupils.

5   **Match the work set with the needs of the pupils.** This means that you need to know not only your subject but also your pupils. Be aware of the breadth of the range of the pupils' abilities. It is then possible to foster high expectations.

6   **Develop effective questioning techniques**. Questioning helps to stretch the pupils by asking them to extend ideas or elaborate on a theme. Verbalising ideas is an effective learning strategy. It also helps teachers to assess the effectiveness of communication in the lesson.

7   **Have detailed plans**. You need both short-term plans for individual lesson and long-term plans for a scheme of work. These in turn needs to fit into overall curriculum planning and examination demands.

8   **Agree clear objectives**. If you are clear about what you want to achieve in any given lesson it is easier to transmit this to the pupils. Once they are aware of the teacher's expectations, they are more likely to succeed. Success breeds success.

9   **Make adequate provision for follow-up**. Be aware that different pupils will want to extend their interest in different directions. Be flexible and have follow-up material for a lot of eventualities.

10 **Share good practice within the department.** Have regular meetings with colleagues in the same subject-specific areas. All members of a department have valuable information and ideas to share. So make sure you build in time to discuss the successes in the department and the lessons and techniques that really worked.

31

Achieving learning for all

In order to achieve learning for all in this era of limited resources it is essential to think of staff development strategies that are cost-effective, both in time and money. Below we list a few tried and tested ideas that other schools have found helpful. All are developmental for the staff and by definition for the pupils too.

1   **Use work shadowing**. This technique allows a teacher to follow another and learn by watching the methods, resources and ideas used by that teacher. This helps one teacher to gain experience and expertise from another.

2   **Share jobs.** This give some members of staff experience in other areas of the school. This can work by delegating responsibility for one aspect of a job to another colleague in the department or school. It can also relieve the pressure on an otherwise overburdened member of staff. This may take the form of allocating library responsibility to a member of staff or giving someone responsibility for exam entries or timetable provision.

3   **Observe others.** To observe a member of staff with expertise in an unfamiliar area is an excellent method of staff development. It can be costly in supply money but allows members of staff to extend their range of techniques and knowledge. Colleagues are often happy to cover for staff in this situation especially if they understand that there will be alternative, reciprocal arrangements for their own development.

4   **Offer short-term contracts.** Give an allowance for a specific internal job for a specific period of time. Again this can be for such things as timetabling, but it can equally be for a particular initiative that has been decided as part of the school development plan.

5   **Rotate responsibility.** This provides an excellent and painless way of giving individuals responsibility for and experience of other tasks in the school. Allocate a responsibility for a fixed term and then allow another person to take on the task for another fixed term. This technique can apply to pastoral roles within the school as well as management responsibility.

6   **Visit other schools.** Where you know of successful innovations or initiatives send a member of staff to observe. Other schools will feel flattered by the recognition of their success and will be only too pleased to show off their successes and skills.

7   **Have an adequate mechanism for the dissemination of information.** Many members of staff have valuable expertise to pass on to others. Devise mechanisms within the school whereby such a person can share this with a group of interested colleagues or with the whole staff. This will be developmental to the person who is passing on the knowledge and will be advantageous to the school as the information is shared and used.

8   **Co-opt members onto the senior management team.** This gives middle management personnel a chance to gain experience related to the wider issues of the school and broadens their perspective. It also give the senior management team other valuable insight and fresh ideas.

9   **Encourage work experience.** Individuals benefit greatly by work experience schemes. Especially if they are complementary to an aspect of their career, they give the participants new perspectives and fresh ideas to bring into the school.

10   **Foster exchanges.** This two-way process allows staff to develop in new directions and bring different ideas into the school and the curriculum.

32

Relationship building

Building relationships is one of the most fundamental skills. A teacher needs to have good relationships with both pupils and colleagues. Fostering good relationships with pupils is essential if trust and a good working environment are to be achieved. It is also as obviously important to be on good terms with colleagues if a productive and cooperative working environment is to be sustained. Good relationships make for a happy school and high-achieving pupils.

1   **Respect others.** Showing respect and valuing someone is very important in fostering good relations. It is as necessary with pupils as it is with adults. Respect helps to build a positive atmosphere. Teachers can no more demand respect from pupils than they can from staff.

2   **Earn respect.** Respect needs to be earned by our behaviour to others. It is necessary to treat others as we would wish to be treated ourselves. Factors such as courtesy and care in building relationships are as important in the workplace as they are with our nearest and dearest at home.

3   **Give positive attention to people**. This means not being distracted. There is nothing worse than feeling that a person is not really listening to and valuing what we say. So try to give a person your full attention. This will show in your body language. For example, eye contact is an important feature in demonstrating that you value a person.

4   **Avoid interrupting.** Try to listen until a person has finished what they are saying. Avoid talking over a person, or interrupting them in order to get in your twopenny-worth. Even if you think your contribution is vitally important, try to contain yourself until the other person has finished what they want to say.

5   **Don't be distracted by other things**. Schools are busy places with constant demands on our attention. There are often many things happening at once. Try to avoid the distraction until the person has finished as this will show that you respect and value their contribution.

6   **Remember pupils' names**. This is one of the hardest things to do, especially when confronted by 30 smiling faces. All are individuals in their own right and all may be desperate for your individual attention. Try to devise some strategy that helps you to remember their names, for example drawing a seating plan or making brief notes on distinguishing marks which can help you remember individuals.

7   **Develop empathy.** This may be a trendy term, but it does appear in a lot of curriculum documents. What it really means is trying to share related experiences with others. If this is not possible we can at least recognise the relevance of the experiences of others.

8   **Be genuine**. Avoid being all things to all people. Try not to run with the hare as well as hunt with the hound. Pupils as well as staff can spot a fake when they see it. If you appear to be putting on a show, it puts people on their guard.

9   **Don't put on an act.** Be yourself. Students respond easily to genuineness. Don't feel you have to set out your stall all the time. You will be better liked and receive genuine response if you are natural, open and simply 'human'.

33

Questioning skills

The skill of asking appropriate questions is crucial to any learning process. Questioning techniques help to direct attention towards pupils' learning. Different types of questioning skills help to identify weaknesses or lack of understanding. Using the appropriate questioning techniques will help to reinforce knowledge and pupils' understanding. It is therefore imperative for any school improvement programme that is centred on improving teaching and learning that staff are aware of the value of different types of questioning. Some of the following ideas might be helpful.

1   **Ask lots and often.** Effective questioning often means that questions are asked frequently. These types of questions are usually simple recall questions and are useful to act as constant reminders. They act as a reinforcement to learning by forcing pupils to stay on task.

2   **Wait for a response.** Give pupils time to think and respond. Don't automatically move to the next person if a response is not immediate. Pupils will learn quickly that they don't have to bother if they know that you will pass them over in search of the right answer from someone else.

3   **Acknowledge correct answers.** When a pupil gives the right answer their success must be acknowledged. Show your appreciation by a smile or a word of praise. This helps pupils to gain confidence, increase motivation and improve morale.

4   **Stick with pupils who give only partial or incorrect answers.** If pupils have only answered part of a question or have not got it quite right, don't pass over to another. Stick with such pupils and encourage them to extend themselves with a complete answer.

5 **Encourage elaboration.** Some pupils are content to give monosyllabic answers. But as teachers who wish to extend learning we should not be. It is helpful to encourage some elaboration. This can be done by using key words or prompts to help pupils to be confident to extend their ideas. Monosyllabic responses may be basically a correct response but it is useful to extend learning by inviting pupils to elaborate their answer and flesh out the detail.

6 **Use open questioning techniques.** Open questioning also encourages elaboration. This technique does not allow the monosyllabic answer. Avoid asking questions that only require a yes-or-no answer. Instead of asking a general question such as, 'Do you know your four-times table?', say instead, 'Tell me the four-times table'.

7 **Avoid closed questions.** Closed questioning should be avoided except for instant reinforcement. Closed questions do not require pupils to think beyond the obvious or the safe. They do not encourage pupils to take risks in their thinking. A closed question could be, 'Did you enjoy that novel?' An open version of the same question would be, 'Tell me what you liked about that novel?'

8 **Ask process questions.** Process questions ask a person to give an opinion, make judgements and offer interpretation. All these encourage thought. They enable pupils to stretch themselves and explore ideas more fully. For example, staying with the novel, you could ask a pupil to explain all the things they liked and disliked about a novel, as well as explaining why they reached that conclusion.

9 **Ask pupils to recall things they should already know.** This type of questioning requires pupils to recall information from a past lesson. This enables pupils to see links between past experience and present learning.

10 **Avoid leading questions.** These suggest certain answers and often lead the pupil into trying to decide what answer the teacher wants, rather than genuinely addressing the question with an open mind.

34

Listening skills

Questioning and listening skills are clearly complementary. It is not only important to ask appropriate questions, it is also essential that a teacher listens attentively to answers. Listening is also a necessary skill for all management and middle management personnel. All interpersonal relationships function more effectively if people feel valued. Most of us spend more time listening than we spend on any other communication activity, but we don't always give the right signals of attention and feedback.

1   **Concentrate on the responses given.** Use eye contact to signal to the person that you are listening not only with your ears but with your whole self. Avoid being distracted. Although this is often difficult in a crowded and active classroom, people do feel valued and respected if they have your attention.

2   **Listen to check understanding.** Only when you listen carefully can you check understanding or ask for clarification of any details. When a person has finished speaking it is helpful to check that you have understood either by asking a question or by making a comment related to what has just been said. If a conversation is one-sided and there is no response it is normal to assume that the other person has not been listening.

3   **Seek elaboration.** Anyone is flattered that their contribution is valued. This is reinforced if you have asked for elaboration of an interesting idea. Pick an interesting point that has been made and ask more about it. This technique is also useful to check understanding.

4   **Confirm that you have understood**. When you have listened carefully you can confirm that you have understood. This can be done by a nod of the head, or better still by making a comment or asking a follow-on question to stretch the speaker further.

5   **Eye contact is important.** Adequate and appropriate eye contact is essential when listening. Avoid continuous eye contact as staring can be off-putting. But it is equally disconcerting for a person to feel that you are not listening because your eyes and attention seem to be elsewhere.

6   **Use appropriate facial gestures.** Appropriate facial gestures communicate responses in the same way as eye contact. Faces communicate in a language that signals subtle responses. Smile occasionally or appropriately. This is far more encouraging than being met by a stone wall of blankness, boredom or distraction.

7   **Don't nod too much.** Although occasional head nodding lets people know that you are listening, beware of nodding too much as it can give the impression of a puppet and is irritating. It often communicates the opposite of attentive listening.

8   **Don't have open ears but a closed mind.** Don't decide too quickly that what a person is saying is going to be boring. When this happens we don't really listen. A glazed expression clouds the eyes. This can give very active signals of boredom and is discouraging to the speaker.

9   **Interpret body language.** Being aware of body language is an important part of developing listening skills. Interpreting non-verbal signals and what they imply are subtle skills that need to be considered.

10 **Have an open body posture.** This implies an open mind and a willingness to listen. Sit facing the other person and avoid curling the body into tight postures. Sit in an upright relaxed manner. For example, crossed legs and folded arms can signal tension and resistance.

35

Giving feedback to pupils and colleagues

Giving feedback effectively is an essential part of any learning process. Giving appropriate feedback to pupils builds confidence and motivation. Feedback also encourages progress as it reinforces existing knowledge. It encourages progression through target-setting for future action. Feedback is also an essential skill in any interviewing process. Most of these tips, therefore, apply equally in a classroom situation as in interviews with adults.

1   **Start with the positive.** Give the positive feedback first. We all like to have our strengths recognised and there is always something worthy of positive comment. This helps to build confidence and create an atmosphere for development.

2   **Avoid listing mistakes.** It is very easy to thoughtlessly provide a list of mistakes to a person. We seem to find it easier, in ourselves as well as others, to look at shortcomings. Even if a person makes a lot of mistakes it is not helpful to dwell on them all. Pick a few important aspects to pass comment on. Prioritise the urgency of the mistakes.

3   **Be specific.** Avoid general comments such as 'That was marvellous'. While generalities may superficially make the person feel good, they are rarely helpful when it comes to development. Specific feedback allows greater opportunity for improvement.

4   **Be constructive.** Constructive feedback does not always imply the positive. However, this should be the first option. But just as it is unhelpful to say something was 'wonderful' so is it unhelpful to say 'That was not very good'. Being specific about exactly what you feel went wrong and what you think can be done to help solve the problem, is the chance to offer some constructive help. Constructive feedback offers ideas to encourage progress or self-awareness.

5   **Use any negative feedback sensitively.** Using negative feedback needs to be done skilfully. It does not imply destructive feedback. When handled sensitively, negative feedback can be a source of suggestions, and provides something to build on.

6   **Offer alternatives.** Offer alternatives by turning a negative into a positive. Only refer to behaviour that can be changed. A person cannot change the shape of their face for instance, but it might be possible to suggest they try to smile a little.

7   **Avoid being over general.** Statements such as 'That was brilliant' or 'You were marvellous' do little to develop skills. Give specific examples of what you thought was 'brilliant' and why. It is especially useful to be specific if you are trying to help a pupil or member of staff to develop a particular skill or extend their knowledge or self-awareness.

8   **Refer only to things that can be changed.** It is useless to say that it is because a person is left-handed that their writing is terrible. It is simpler and more productive to suggest that they practise handwriting skills in order to make their work legible.

9   **Begin feedback with 'in my opinion'.** This avoids giving the impression that we are the fount of all knowledge. This gives the person the option whether to accept your opinion or not.

10   **Listen to our own feedback.** If we listen to the feedback we give to others it can tell us a lot about our own value system. Listening to oneself helps any individual to realise what they need to focus on and it is an important developmental tool to self-knowledge.

36

Receiving feedback

For any personal development it is important to know how others experience us. When we receive feedback it is part of the learning process. It helps us acknowledge our strengths and gain confidence through them. It also helps us to recognise the effect we have on others and where behaviour modification or skills improvement are needed. Feedback guides effective learning. Looking at the way we receive feedback assists development in a twofold manner. It allows us not only to alter our behaviour as a result of particular feedback, but it also allows us to alter the way we give feedback to others in the light of being on the receiving end. The following tips are aimed at members of staff, but apply equally to the way in which students receive feedback

1   **Be polite and listen.** Feedback can be uncomfortable to hear and our instinct is often to find an excuse to leave, or to switch off. But it is still possible to be polite. Feedback is usually given with the best of motives. People do really feel they are trying to help.

2   **Don't immediately reject the feedback.** The natural reaction is to try to justify our own actions or thoughts. It is very threatening to feel that we are being criticised. Don't immediately argue about the feedback. Other opinions are valid (but it is useful to remember that they are only the opinions of one other person).

3   **Feel free to accept or reject feedback.** (After you have listened to it, of course!) Teachers try to offer sound advice based on knowledge and experience. But you are still a free person and it is only one person's viewpoint. Seek a second opinion if you feel unhappy.

4   **Make sure you understand the feedback.** Beware of misunderstanding. Since receiving feedback can sometimes be sensitive, we can filter our understanding. When any point is ambiguous or unclear, ask for details to clarify what you think was said or suggested.

5   **Summarise the feedback.** It is useful to offer a summary of your perception of the feedback you have just received. This clears up any misunderstandings. Both people are then clear about what has been said and understood.

6   **Don't necessarily accept one person's view**. Hospitals and doctors' waiting rooms are full of people seeking a second opinion. This is particularly true in the realm of health as the issues at stake are crucial to life. But your career is also a major part of your life and your development is just as important as your health. So check it out with others.

7   **Use the feedback to help your development.** Feedback, however painful and difficult, is usually developmental. This may not always be obvious at the time. But lick the wounds, they heal very quickly.

8   **Make your own decisions.** After receiving feedback it is up to you how much you accept and how much you reject the observations made. Again it is important not to take everything too seriously. Filter what has been said, take on board what you can change and leave the rest on hold. You can't change everything at once and some things you will never be able to change. So take a pragmatic approach to your own development before you jump off the bridge!

9   **Action plan.** After an interview or an appraisal, or in the classroom, the process of receiving feedback enables individuals to prioritise needs and plan for development. Again be pragmatic, go for what is achievable and don't waste time on the fanciful.

10 **Set your own targets**. Having heard feedback you are in a better position to set targets for yourself. Your strengths have been acknowledged and your weaknesses probably confirmed – but at least you know. Make knowing yourself a priority. If, after all this feedback, you don't, something has gone badly wrong somewhere!

37

Recording skills

The recording of information is a vital part of any school activity. It allows us to refer to documents for accuracy. It is also essential in any assessment process. It enables benchmarks to be set on present performance and targets for planning future school improvement. Records need to be kept as part of a formative process. They allow schools to be accountable for their actions and to assist monitoring and planning progress. The usefulness of keeping records, however, is dependent on the extent to which records are used. This is as true at the individual pupil level as well as at the school level. It is no use having mountains of paper that no one consults.

1   **Records should provide a useful basis for reports.** This does not mean only formal reports to parents. Other teachers need reports as do pupils themselves. But records and comments need to be contextualised otherwise they can be fairly meaningless.

2   **Highlight causes for concern or praise.** Of course record-keeping is to assist in learning by highlighting concern. But if all the comments are negative this can be counter-productive. It can be also a great motivator if records are consciously used as a mechanism for praise.

3   **Use records to facilitate the planning of future work.** Records help at school, departmental and individual levels to inform future planning for improvement. Schools have a great deal of data readily available, for example attendance records and exam results, to name but two. These existing statutory records can be used to set benchmarks and targets for future improvement.

4   **Have a consistent marking policy.** In relation to recording and reporting pupils' progress, it is essential to have a coherent and consistent marking policy. A school needs to have a whole school policy on recording achievement. These policy statements need to be set within the context of clearly stated purposes. Just as you do when identifying assessment needs, ask what you should record, how you should record it and who will use the information.

5   **Recognise necessary variations of approach.** While there needs to be whole school principles, in relation to record-keeping different departments will have different approaches. These different needs must be set within the broad principles of intent throughout the school.

6   **Have a range of recording methods**. Oral assessments need a different method of recording to a more straightforward mark-on-a-scale approach. Written comments are often of more use than raw scores that only an individual knows the value of.

7   **Promote internal activities to help with consistency.** Where possible, particularly within a department, devise some common assignments or activities that enable standardisation meetings. This helps promote consistency.

8   **Have inter-school standardisation meetings.** Inter-school activities are of especial importance to assist in transition from one Key Stage to another. If records are to be understood when passed on to another school, there must be a consistent approach. Otherwise no one will make sense of records from partner and feeder schools and you will have no baseline from which to work.

9   **Use records to support curriculum reviews.** Use assessment outcomes to inform reviews of curriculum provision and the effectiveness of teaching. Within any curriculum area, masses of information is collected about pupils. This information should be sifted and focused to allow important issues to be addressed regarding school improvement.

10 **Use subject-specific National Curriculum guidelines.** All National Curriculum stages offer guidelines for assessing and recording. They can provide tools for recording work effectively.

38

Negotiation skills

In any negotiation, outcomes will depend on the relationship already established between the two (or more) people. The negotiation referred to here (we hope) bears little relationship to popularised confrontational negotiations related to pay bargaining or industrial disputes. However, the skills involved are not dissimilar. The key element within any successful negotiation is trust.

1 **Use empathy.** This may be an over-used word, but it is useful to try to put ourselves into another person's shoes. This helps to avoid the bully or be bullied syndrome. If we are able to put ourselves in the other's place, we will avoid inflicting our ideas and preconceptions onto them.

2 **Avoid making assumptions about others.** Try to approach any negotiation with an open mind. There may have been rumours on the grapevine that you are not happy about, or you may have clashed swords before, but clear your mind of any previous encounters. Try to start each negotiation with a clean slate.

3 **Try to ensure equal participation.** All negotiation needs to be two-way. Make sure that there is equal time for both parties to express their views. Don't hog the floor. Make sure that no one is a loser; seek compromises where necessary, so that all parties have tangible positive outcomes.

4 **Use active listening skills genuinely.** Use all your listening skills, including those related to body language. Have your antennae well tuned to respond to all nuances.

5 **Ensure that what you say is understood.** It is useful for both parties to summarise what they feel has been the content of the debate, and any agreements reached. This will avoid any later misunderstanding as to the content of the negotiation.

6   **Be enthusiastic.** Try to convey your interest and enthusiasm. Be positive about jobs or tasks done well and improvements made. We usually remember to be enthusiastic with pupils but often forget with adults.

7   **Generate a variety of options**. Before coming to a final decision ensure that the maximum number of options has been explored. These options can be general or specific, but will need to be narrowed before any final agreements are reached.

8   **Look for mutual gains**. It is possible, and probably essential, to look for ways of pleasing each party. If a colleague has an enthusiastic but unrealistic idea in relation to some form of change, try to harness the enthusiasm while modifying the idea. Try to assess issues on their merits rather than engage in any form of haggling.

9   **Make sure that both parties agree.** At least, carry on negotiating till there are significant areas of agreement, even if some matters remain unresolved. Without the agreement of both parties there is little hope of development or change, and outcomes will merely have lip service paid to them, and nothing concrete will happen.

10 **Reach an agreement that is satisfactory to the school as well as the individual.** It is essential in relation to written school policies and Statements of Principle that any agreement reached is within the context of these documents and is for the benefit of both parties. Staff development and training should be within the context of the needs of the school as well as the needs of the individual. For example, it would normally be impractical to spend staff development allocations on the whim of an English teacher who suddenly wished to read for a biology degree. The school will probably already have good biology teachers and that particular degree will do little to enhance the teaching of English.

Chapter 6 Training Delivery

We have already looked in broad terms at staff development. Now we look more specifically at one of the principal means of achieving focused staff development: training. We start with some suggestions about setting appropriate targets. If the targets are seen as worthwhile and achievable, there is much more likelihood that everyone will pull together to turn them into realities.

We move on to suggestions about running a successful training day. It is not enough that everyone gets together and wrestles with the issues of the day; a successful training day has to be planned in considerable detail, yet retain flexibility to deal with matters arising when these are really important. It is best to plan a training day in terms of what colleagues will *do* from minute to minute, not in terms merely of what they will hear about.

Sometimes it is best to bring in a trainer from outside the school. This can be particularly useful when you may need the person taking the lead at a training event to be seen as neutral or impartial on touchy issues. However, the success of such training events depends a lot on your choice of trainer, and on how well you brief the trainer on the local context. To get the best results from external trainers, you need to make them feel valued and respected, and it is worth going to some lengths to make the day as trouble-free as possible for them. We offer our suggestions, many of which have been learned from training days that went wrong!

Training outcomes depend a lot on what happened on the day, but even more on what happens *after* the day. Our final set of suggestions in this chapter is about ways of ensuring that training is followed up by appropriate, focused action. After all, school improvement is not measured in terms of people who *know* what to do to implement changes, but in terms of the changes that are implemented, and the evidence that proves this to have been achieved.

39

Identifying appropriate training targets

The purpose of training is to enable change and development to occur. For this to happen effectively, both the school and the individual need to know as much as possible about the priorities for implementing improvements. The following suggestions should help you to ensure that your training targets are useful and appropriate.

1   **Targets should be SMART.** It can't be said too often that targets for training and school improvement need to be Specific, Measurable, Achievable, Realistic and Time-constrained.

2   **Targets should be rigorous**. It is no use setting broad general targets, or targets that you know are easy to achieve. Targets need to be a genuine training and developmental device. Stretch yourself, otherwise there is no point in doing it.

3   **Targets should be related to departmental and school development plans.** Much emphasis needs to be laid on the necessary link between individual development and whole school planning. Without this connection, any training can do little to improve the quality of teaching and learning and therefore offers little in the way of school improvement.

4   **Targets should be monitored**. When targets are set and training needs identified, there should be a system in place to monitor and evaluate the effectiveness of the training, whether it is individual training or that designed to meet whole school developmental plans.

5   **Targets should be evaluated**. In order to evaluate the effectiveness of any training, performance indicators need to be identified and benchmarks established. These provide a point from which to measure success. By continuous measurement of the performance indicators, it is possible to plot the rate of change, using IT packages where appropriate.

6   **Targets should be challenging.** Just as we challenge pupils to extend their skills and knowledge, so should staff training seek to broaden vision and encourage change. If staff find the targets relevant and realistic, and have a sense of ownership of them, even the most challenging of such targets can be met.

7   **Targets should make a difference.** Targets should affect what happens in the day-to-day life of the school. Targets should be practical and seek to bring about some change in an individual's performance or in the organisational structure of a school. They should lead to an improvement to some aspect of life in the school.

8   **Targets should improve the quality of teaching.** Schools are about pupils and improving the quality of their education. Teaching skills are the most fundamental resource that the school has to offer. Therefore, all targets should have some visible connection to the quality of teaching in the school.

9   **Targets should improve the quality of learning**. Pupils have a right to a good education. Teachers have a responsibility to enhance and improve the quality of pupils' learning. All training targets should relate directly to the quality of pupils' learning in one way or another.

10 **Targets should improve school effectiveness.** If training needs are identified, and targets are set within the context of agreed principles and agreed developmental plans, by definition they must improve the effectiveness of the school. If targets are set with pupils in mind, the quality of teaching and learning are bound to be enhanced.

40

Planning a training day

Training days are wonderful opportunities to enable staff to get together and work on current issues within a school. They can also be a terrible waste of time and effort where they are disorganised and lack focus. These tips aim to help you plan and organise a day that makes people feel as if they have spent their time productively.

1   **Have a clear set of aims for the day.** Training events are more likely to be successful if everyone can see the purpose of them, and all concerned openly recognise that the goals set are worthwhile.

2   **Share the responsibility for organising the day.** Don't let the responsibility for every aspect of the day fall to one person. By sharing out the workload, you are likely to increase the ownership the participants will have of the outcomes of the day.

3   **Think carefully about your venue.** If you stay in school, there is a danger that people will find it all to easy to be called back to their normal roles. If you go off site, there will normally be quite high expenses associated with the event, but the facilities may be better. Staff may well like to feel a bit pampered, but may get rebellious if they feel money is being needlessly spent when it could be better used elsewhere.

4   **Organise your equipment and resources.** A standard pack might include: overhead projector; spare transparencies and pens; flipchart stand with pad and pens; pencils and paper; Post-its; scissors; Blu-Tack or masking tape.

5   **Make sure you have all the right documentation with you.** It is frustrating if people fail to bring with them key documents needed for planning and review, so it is as well to remind them (and bring spare back-up copies).

6   **Plan the shape of the day productively.** Be realistic about how long you will need for refreshment breaks, especially if participants are likely to have to walk any distance for refreshments or if queuing is necessary. You can guarantee rebellion if your breaks are not long enough to permit the smokers to get outside and have a cigarette!

7   **Build in activities.** Although some people like to listen to an expert, you cannot expect all participants to give their best if they have to spend too long listening without participating. Aim to break up the sessions with pair and small-group activities, just as you would with pupils. Balance is the important principle.

8   **Try to ensure that minority as well as majority views are heard and recorded.** If you want participants to feel committed to school improvement, you need to ensure that they don't feel railroaded or ignored. Sometimes people making an objection are perfectly satisfied once the objection is recorded in an appropriate way.

9   **At the end of the day, plan for future action.** If all the goals of the day have not yet been achieved, try to reach agreement about who will do what, by when. Encourage people to think about the barriers that will stop them from undertaking the follow-up tasks, and to look for strategies to get round them. As far as possible, get individuals and small groups to commit to definite courses of action, with deadlines.

10   **Ensure that the event finishes smoothly.** Try to avoid having people just drifting away at the end of the day to other commitments. Try to negotiate a clear finishing time to which participants can commit themselves, and then stick to it absolutely. Never overrun.

41

Choosing and using external trainers

With budgetary constraints, training is often conducted inhouse using the expertise of your own staff. However, there are times when it is useful to bring in an authoritative voice from outside. Even if the messages to be delivered are similar, an outside expert can often add gravitas or a new perspective. Here are some suggestions for choosing and using trainers from outside.

1   **Choose your trainer carefully.** Probably the best way is through personal recommendations: find someone who you have heard is good and use them. Remember that the most expensive trainer is not necessarily the best but that good trainers tend to be very busy and ration by price. Be suspicious of very cheap trainers who are too available. You might ask why they aren't getting a lot of work!

2   **Plan well ahead.** To get the venue and the trainer you want, you will need to have a lead time of several months. Avoid rushing round at the last minute. This will result in getting someone who is available, rather than the best expert in the field. If possible, meet the person in advance and help them plan a programme to incorporate their own strengths which also meet the school's needs.

3   **Check the real price for the job.** Make sure you know whether you are responsible for travel, accommodation, subsistence and VAT as well as the agreed fee. If these are not agreed in advance, there can be embarrassment later. Check early whether they are self-employed and whether tax should be deducted at source from the fee. In the UK, make sure you have their National Insurance number and other relevant details, without which your funding authority may not pay them.

4   **Brief your trainer fully.** Good trainers know that every context is different, so try to let them know as much as is relevant about your school, your staff and your needs in advance. In that way, you are more likely to get a focused workshop that satisfies your requirements, rather than something generic or off-the-shelf.

5   **Check out precisely what the trainer needs.** Send a map well in advance so they can find the venue, and ask what they need in the way of equipment and materials. If they want you to copy handouts, ask for them to be supplied in time for your school's reprographics staff (if you have them) to deal with them, so you are not standing over a hot photocopier yourself at the last minute.

6   **Look after the trainer**. Workshops usually work best if you make the trainer feel valued. Is it possible for someone to meet the trainer from the station or provide transport from the hotel? Can you provide an easy-to-find parking space? Offer a warm drink on arrival, especially if there has been a long journey and help with checks that everything is in place that is needed. Show where the toilets are, and provide water during the session. It can be thirsty work training!

7   **Introduce the trainer properly.** An endorsement from someone senior can help staff value the session, but ensure that the introducer is well briefed. Most trainers have a two or three sentence 'blurb' about themselves they will give you on request.

8   **Monitor the trainer's performance.** If you want to know whether you are getting value for money and whether your staff are getting something out of the session, you will need to participate yourself. Many commissioners of training make the mistake of thinking that all they have to do is set the event up and leave it to run itself. It is usually best if someone senior is on hand to sort out problems when they arise, and give a local context when necessary.

9   **Evaluate the training**. Use an evaluation form, asking participants to write open comments on a sheet of paper or on Post-its. It is also useful simply to go round the circle of participants, asking them what the best thing about the training session has been.

10 **Close the session well.** Thank the trainer, help with the clearing up and see them on their way home. Reflect for a while on what are likely to be the main outcomes for the day, note any action points that have been agreed and think through how these will be followed up.

42

Following up training

On occasions, it happens that everyone goes away from a training day feeling fired up and enthusiastic, ready to get down to a whole series of tasks to help make real improvements. Weeks or months later people realise nothing has happened and say, 'Well, it didn't really achieve much, did it?' The fault might not lie with the day itself, but with the lack of follow-up. These tips aim to prevent this happening by helping you to plan post-event action.

1   **Make sure that action planning is part of every training day.** This needs to be done in a way where everyone identifies exactly what they plan to do at once, then in the short term, then in the longer term, and where all such resolutions are written down and shared.

2   **Build in an action planning review.** After a busy training day, there may not be much time or energy for discussing and sharing action plan ideas. It is then worth setting aside time for a short post-training get-together of everyone who took part, to explain to each other (and fine-tune) their plans for implementing the outcomes of the training.

3   **Keep records of actions people have promised to make.** Ideally circulate these to all participants as soon as possible after the training day is over so that participants cannot afterwards claim to have no recollection of them.

4   **Design a simple form for everyone to complete about 'actions taken so far'.** Make this short and sharp, with a deadline for submission. Just having such a form to fill in can be a spur to actually getting down to some actions regarding implementing things learned from a training session.

5   **Feed individual targets into staff development programmes.** Link the targets set by individuals in their appraisals into your training programme. Patterns of training needs will emerge from this. Providing these are reviewed by the staff development coordinator, these targets can fuel action planning for training.

6   **Get participants to act as each other's progress chasers.** If possible, get them to work in pairs, with reports on progress at regular intervals. Peer support and encouragement is often more successful in getting people to do things than an authoritarian approach.

7   **When individuals or teams succeed in reaching their targets, circulate information about them.** This may jog the memories and spur the consciences of those who have not yet made a start on their own. It also gives those who have worked hard credit for their efforts.

8   **Keep a progress chart for a clear overall picture of task achievement.** When lots of people are working on parallel tasks, it is easy to lose sight of the general plan. Something visual, placed in a position where people see it frequently, can help to ensure that the 'broad picture' is not lost by anyone.

9   **Be realistic about parts of action plans that are not achieved.** There may be good reasons for this happening; for example, there may be further training needs that can be identified from those areas in which progress seems to be slow. Rather than blaming staff for not achieving their targets, ask them about what further training could help them.

10   **Be ready to fine-tune and renegotiate action plans.** It often happens that something that seemed straightforward at the planning stage is more difficult to implement in practice. Legitimise and recognise this possibility by planning renegotiation slots in the action plans.

Chapter 7 Appraisal

School improvement necessarily involves the use of an effective appraisal system. It can ensure achievements are recorded and commended, shortfalls can be noted and pains taken to remedy them, and training requirements identified and matched to whole school and local departmental needs. This chapter explores ways in which appraisal can be used as a dynamic agent for personal performance enhancement and development, so as to contribute to school improvement overall.

We start with some suggestions for self-appraisal. This can not only be useful preparation for formal appraisal interviews, but can be a vital ongoing process for keeping a sense of perspective about how you are addressing your own career development in the context of the changes involved in school improvement. The techniques an individual uses in self-appraisal are identical in essence to those used when conducting whole school reviews or curriculum audits and will similarly be ongoing, cyclical and subject to continuous modification and review.

Next, we look at some of the aspects of teaching that may form important parts of the appraisal agenda. Addressing these aspects helps appraisal to be a positive influence in the development of classroom performance by teachers, and also addresses the needs of pupils as learners.

Our next set of recommendations is about arriving at an appropriate and realistic focus for appraisal. The purposes need to be clear, the targets need to be realistic, and the agenda needs to be relevant and well articulated. We follow this with more detailed advice on individual target-setting.

Appraisal should not be a paper-based exercise, but needs to be centred on evidence and action. Our suggestions for maximising the effectiveness of appraisal may help to optimise the benefits it can deliver.

The next set of suggestions is about how to bring the findings of appraisal processes into the broader picture of the professional development of the staff in general, and the specific personal development of individual members of staff within a school improvement programme.

43

Fostering effective
self-appraisal

Critical self-review is the first step in any appraisal system. It is also a necessary ingredient for any personal development. Without a self-review there can be neither individual improvement nor school improvement. Self-appraisal is, therefore, a valuable process, not only as preparation for an individual's appraisal process, but as an ongoing, and continuous part of improving teaching and learning skills. The following are prompts to help reflection on current work and practices.

1   **What aspects of your work do you feel are successful?** It is always good to start with the positive. It makes us feel confident to reflect on our successes. As teachers we find it easy to look at what went wrong but often do not reward ourselves with congratulations on our achievements.

2   **Which aspects of your work are less successful?** Move from the comfort zone of the positive 'feel good' factor to looking at what has not been quite as successful as we would have liked. Begin with broad questions to start you thinking and analysing your work. It will help later when trying to arrive at a focus for development.

3   **Look at your job description.** This is a good time to decide if it is accurate and encompasses all your tasks and responsibilities. There may be things you want to add as you have taken on responsibilities since your last appraisal. Equally, you may have embarked on an initiative that is now complete, so you might need to amend the document.

4   **Set and prioritise aims and objectives**. When you have drawn up a list of possible areas of interest for change and development, it is useful to categorise these objectives into short and long term. You won't be able to do them all, but prioritising them helps you to start with the most important.

5   **Draw up a programme of activities.** This programme should meet the objectives set. Again, divide this into a short- and long-term programme. Decide on the most important and put those in the short-term plan and put the others on hold for longer-term plans. But do set yourself time targets otherwise the longer-term activities have a habit of disappearing into the calendars of science fiction.

6   **Devise simple criteria for checking the standards.** Your success can then be measured against benchmarks. Too often, people set themselves vague and woolly targets and then find it difficult to ascertain whether they have been reached or not.

7   **Evaluate your effectiveness.** All aspects of appraisal need to be evaluated. Test the effectiveness of your work against the criteria you have devised. Be realistic without beating yourself up!

8   **What prevented you?** Ask yourself what stopped you from achieving any of the targets you set yourself. You may then need to modify the targets into a more realistic framework, or it may mean devising whole new structures and plans.

9   **What changes do I need to make?** All school improvement ultimately rests with what is happening in the classroom. Improved teaching and learning stems from the teacher on the 'chalk-face', so ask yourself what you can do to improve your own performance in the classroom.

10 **What changes can there be in the school organisation?** Broaden your perspective into a whole school context. Ask yourself what else would be beneficial to help you to improve your performance.

44

Improving skills and performance through appraisal

During self-appraisal, teachers will have examined their teaching methods, their strengths and their weaknesses. Teachers will also find it helpful to use the observation component of appraisal as a means of identifying and improving their skills in the classroom. Listed below are some of the possible areas that might be observed in order to improve performance in the classroom. They may be useful at the self-appraisal stage of the process or in later stages when you are choosing a focus for observation or future targets for action. During the self-appraisal process, or before an observation, it may be useful to ask yourself about some of the following areas of your classroom work.

1 **Use a variety and range of materials in any given lesson.** Most schools have a variety of resources to fit individual needs. Avoid using the same types of stimulus material. You will get bored and so will the pupils.

2 **Use a range of approaches.** It is useful to vary approaches in lessons. If pupils feel that they always do things in the same way, using the same method and the same type of resources, they will quickly become bored. While it may give the teacher confidence, through familiarity, to use some tried-and-tested method, it can be death to the imagination and to pupil involvement.

3 **Look for pupils' involvement in tasks.** Participation in discussion is one indicator of pupil involvement. The level of pupils' involvement in the task set will help to determine motivation. Ask pupils to explain the task. This will help to determine if the pupils are interested and know what is expected of them. Clear understanding of tasks helps pupils achieve the desired learning outcomes.

4   **Make sure the physical layout of the room is appropriate for the learning activity.** Are there displays of pupils' work on the walls? Displays provide stimulus for activities. Is the seating appropriate for the activity? Decide in advance what type of activity you will be doing and try to make the physical layout appropriate.

5   **Make sure pupils know what behaviour is expected.** This involves inappropriate behaviour being responded to effectively. It is also helpful to have a consistent programme of sanctions and rewards.

6   **Maintain a working atmosphere.** This is achieved through appropriate communication. A teacher needs to make clear the structure and purpose of any learning experience; this helps to keep pupils on task.

7   **Have clear – and high – expectations of outcomes.** In any curriculum planning, expectations of outcomes and the means of assessing those outcomes should be built into schemes of work. Pupils respond to clear instructions and clear guidelines of what they are being asked to achieve.

8   **Make sure there is adequate planning and preparation.** Pupils should be aware of how their work fits into a scheme or structured course. Progression needs to be built into the activities and tasks.

9   **Have clear goals for each lesson.** If you have clear goals you can communicate them to pupils. They will then feel more secure. To communicate those goals make clear the structure and purpose of the learning experience. This again adds to security. It provides better motivation to pupils. Pupils are more likely to succeed if they know where they are going and how the work fits into a pattern.

10 **Build in assessment mechanisms.** Some form of record-keeping system should be in place to evaluate, give feedback and plan for future development. Pupils should also be aware of the assessment criteria for any given lesson. Don't assess everything. Be selective, assess what is important.

45

Arriving at a focus

After any process of self-appraisal you will be aware of areas for change and personal development, but arriving at a focus for classroom observation in any individual appraisal should be a matter of discussion between the appraiser and appraisee. However, it is often one of the most difficult areas in which to make a useful and productive decision. Much of the later advice in relation to setting targets is relevant here. It can be easier to decide on a classroom focus once you have a general idea of your targets for action, change and development. Whichever way round you choose to come to a decision, discussions should be within the context of any whole school issues and departmental priorities that have been decided, as well as any considerations for your personal development.

1   **Try not to simply play safe.** In the first cycles of appraisal many teachers chose the safe option. As confidence builds teachers become more experimental. Playing safe is rarely developmental and does little to improve teaching or learning.

2   **Don't be too cautious.** Don't be afraid to raise important professional issues. This will provide a real opportunity for development. It avoids classroom observations merely being an affirmative exercise. If the relationship is good between appraiser and appraisee it will be easier to decide on a focus for observation that will lead to some genuine development.

3   **Focus on an area that you need to improve.** This is much easier if the appraiser and appraisee have a good relationship. When this is so appraisal offers an excellent opportunity to work in confidence with a trusted colleague. Since appraisal should be a genuine opportunity for development and change, don't waste it in cosy comfort zones or back patting.

4   **Teaching is your job**. It seems appropriate that at least one of the areas of focus for appraisal is on classroom skills. You may do it well but you can always improve. It is in the classroom that effective teaching and learning counts.

5   **Have two or more focuses.** Since it is important to marry the needs of the school and the needs of the individual, it follows that in a lot of cases there will need to be more than one area of focus. This means that one focus can be a classroom focus and the other can concentrate on a whole school issue or another aspect of a teacher's work.

6   **Choose an area that benefits both the school and the individual**. Appraisal should be developmental for all concerned. It therefore makes sense in every way to link the needs of the individual with the needs of the school. Don't be appraised in isolation.

7   **At least one focus needs to be linked to school development plans**. School development planning should have been conducted in a consultative manner. When this happens, it will be easy for any individual to link an area of focus to the school or departmental development plans.

8   **Try the competency approach.** This may be an emotive subject. But the Teacher Training Agency (TTA) has guidelines for training new teachers using competence-based appraisal. We assess pupil by giving clear criteria. So why not assess teachers in a similar way?

9   **Use prompt lists.** The Department for Education and Employment (DfEE) has published an extensive list of competences. Many schools have adapted these for their own use. Other schools have devised their own in a consultative way with their staff.

10 **Learn from the first cycle**. Schools are now past the first nervous phases of appraisal. Use the experience gained and the mistakes made to find a more efficient and effective way of determining an area of focus.

46

Target-setting for teachers

Professional targets for improvement, whether set solely by the individual or whether negotiated as part of a school development plan, are an essential ingredient if any school improvement is to take place. Targets are part of a school's development plan as well as the staff development plan. It is often helpful to prioritise the targets into short-term and long-term objectives and to set a timescale for achievement and review. Targets need not be set in tablets of stone; they should be part of a continual evaluation and reviewing process. We start with the oft repeated advice that targets must therefore be SMART and then list a few other ideas to help in the process of target-setting, whether at the personal level of an appraisal cycle or at the whole school level of development planning and school improvement.

1   **Targets should be specific.** Avoid broad general targets as they often prove meaningless in reality. Broad generalisations are very hard to pin down or use to devise any evaluation techniques with which to assess achievement.

2   **Devise some criteria so that targets are measurable**. If targets are not specific it will be more difficult to find any benchmarks or devise any performance indicators to evaluate success. Ask the questions, 'How can I know if I have been successful?', 'What measurement can I use to indicate the degree of success I have achieved?'

3   **Make sure that your targets are achievable.** If your targets are both specific and measurable, and you have devised a way of evaluating success, it is far more likely you will achieve what you set out to do. It is also helpful to think carefully about the context and timescale of your targets.

4   **Targets need to be realistic.** Don't be too ambitious. Keep your targets to something you know you can achieve. This is also helped by the fact that they will already be specific, and that you will have already considered how you are going to evaluate that success. These exercises will help assist in weeding out the more unrealistic elements in your target-setting.

5   **Put you targets within a timescale.** This means that you will have a definite period in which to achieve success. Without this timescale, things get bypassed and overlooked in the busy day-to-day life of teaching.

6   **Define some performance indicators.** You will have already started to consider ways of evaluating your performance and success in the earlier stages of considering your target-setting. Without some specific means of measuring outcomes it is difficult to monitor progress.

7   **Make your targets developmental.** Appraisal is part of your personal development programme as well as the school's, so try to think of areas of your teaching or in your other responsibilities that will be developmental for you. By definition, this should also be of benefit to the school. If you don't stretch yourself there will be little improvement.

8   **Targets should also be relevant.** Make sure that your targets have some bearing on your present job or future aspirations. They should fit into the overall development objectives of the school, but they should also fit into the plans of the curriculum and improved teaching and learning.

9   **Try to challenge yourself.** Most people like a good challenge, especially when they are competing against their own targets.

10 **Set targets that you feel you will enjoy.** It is not always true that the bitterest pill is the most effective. There is often more success when the pill is sweet.

47

Maximising the effectiveness of appraisal

In order to maximise the effectiveness of appraisal it must be linked to whole school development planning as well as to the demands of departmental plans (which in turn should be linked to school plans). It is essential to have a clarity and coherence in professional development policies. These policies need to be devised in the context of a consultation process that enables all staff to participate and agree in order to feel ownership of these policies and strategies. If there is little or no consultation there will be little or no cooperation.

1   **Establish some school-wide targets.** Use the school's development plan to establish some whole school targets that can be adapted by departments and individuals. This allows everyone in the school to incorporate at least one of the school's targets in their individual appraisal. It can make it easier for some members of staff to chose a focus for their classroom observation if they are able to link it to an established and agreed school or departmental target.

2   **Make sure that staff development policies are clear to all staff.** The policies should also include a statement explaining the criteria for allocating resources, both in terms of time and money.

3   **Establish formal channels of communication.** This will enable staff who prefer to have structures to know exactly how to channel their information into the appraisal system. Some members of staff work well within an ad hoc or personality cult situation, but most feel isolated and rejected without adequate and understood structures.

4   **Do not leave appraisal statements sitting unnoticed in the filing cabinet.** In a busy school it is easy to pay lip service to the appraisal system with pieces of paper to prove that it has been done. But if statements are never looked at or followed up staff lose confidence in what should be a major system of staff development. Staff feel insulted if they think that their appraisal statement and targets have been left unnoticed.

5   **Feed individual targets into the whole staff development system.** This is usually done through the staff development officer. The staff development coordinator can then spot trends, prioritise needs and devolve expenditure.

6   **Set aside funding for meeting appraisal needs**. This is usually done within the school's staff development budget and has been decided under some rational principles rather than an ad hoc system based on who is the most vociferous member of staff.

7   **Coordinators should ensure that appraisers are well briefed about their role.** This should include a knowledge of the school's professional development policies, its short- and long-term targets and its priorities.

8   **Make sure that all staff understand the school development plan.** This is usually best achieved when staff have been involved in some way in the process of compiling the document.

9   **Set up a staff development committee.** This helps, especially in a large school where communication is more difficult. Committees allow people who would not normally be involved to feel that their opinion is valued. Small groups are often more productive. They can feed back their discussions to the full staff for consideration.

10   **Have an open style of management.** This enables individuals to participate and feel ownership of school policies. This in turn will clearly lead to more cooperation and thus be more effective.

48

Identifying potential professional development

Appraisal should be an extremely effective mechanism for identifying individual needs for professional development. These individual needs can then be incorporated into an overall staff development programme and linked with departmental or whole school planning. Appraisal can often also unlock previously untapped potential in all staff. Staff are the largest most comprehensive resource that a school has. There is often a lot of hidden potential for school improvement. It is essential to harness those ideas (and the expertise highlighted during the appraisal process) to benefit both the school and the individual, and by extension, the pupils.

1   **Locate staff development in the classroom.** Effective teaching and learning take place in the classroom. Without effective teaching and learning it is difficult for any school improvement to take place.

2   **Use the appraisal system to identify the needs of staff.** The confidentiality clause in appraisal can be too rigidly adhered to. The targets set in any appraisal interview should be seen and used by the staff development coordinator. Targets can be used to identify individual staff development needs as well as any whole school issues that are repeatedly highlighted.

3   **Feed individual targets into the staff development plan.** For an effective staff development programme, individual targets need to be given to the staff development coordinator, and then fed into future staff development planning.

4   **Identify patterns of need by using the appraisal statements.** Patterns of concern, even though located in different areas of the school, may often become articulated during the appraisal cycle. The staff development coordinator can incorporate these needs into future staff development plans.

5   **Allow some flexibility in the budget.** Although a lot of staff development needs can be met inhouse, they still require budgeting in terms of time management. If external trainers are needed, this will have to be budgeted for.

6   **Improve skills and performance through appraisal.** Setting a particular focus during the observation component in the appraisal cycle allows teachers to improve their skills in certain areas of their work.

7   **All targets should go to the staff development coordinator.** The staff development coordinator should read carefully all targets set during an appraisal which allows planning to take place in terms of the training and development needs of the whole school as well as of individual teachers.

8   **Appraisers can identify the strengths and weaknesses.** During classroom observation strengths can be identified. These strengths can then be used to help others. Any weaknesses can be supported with staff development initiatives and planning.

9   **Use the skills demonstrated in one section of the school to develop and extend the teaching skills in other areas.** Where you have a strong department, with innovative or successful ideas and methods, provide a structure to allow those skills to be shared. An example of this might be for a member of the languages department to visit the drama department to develop skills in role-play teaching techniques – a skill used in both disciplines.

10   **Individual needs and departmental needs should be fed into school development.** Put in place a communication mechanism whereby the needs identified during appraisal can be fed into the system. Without this type of communication framework a lot of potential for staff development will be lost.

Chapter 8 Closing The Quality Loop

We end with suggestions on 'closing the quality loop', aiming to provide a sharp checklist of questions, for which there should be agreed and firm answers, when the school improvement plan is in place.

In order for there to be a successful whole school plan for quality improvement, it's a good idea to include everyone involved. This section of tips is designed to help you think about how you can make sure that all facets of the school are brought in to a continuous process of involvement. Here is a set of questions you could ask.

1 **Is everyone on board?** Do all categories of staff employed in the school know about plans for school improvement and embrace them? Is the policy public and overt? Is it accessible and written in language that everyone can understand?

2 **Are the ancillary staff involved?** Does everyone, including cleaners, catering staff, classroom supporters, lollipop people and others, know what you are trying to achieve, and have they been invited to think how they can contribute to it?

3 **Are the governors involved?** Do they do more than rubber stamp the plans? Do they have the chance to make suggestions, comment on drafts, and add the views of the wider community?

4 **Are the pupils involved?** They don't have to be bored with the full details (although some might like access to them). Do they understand why there is a plan for school improvement, and are they encouraged to invest in it?

5 **Is the library/resource centre geared up to school improvement?** When resources are tight, this can be problematic, but are people working there aware of the plans and looking for creative, visionary and cost-effective ways to support them?

6   **Do you have contingency plans for when things go wrong?** Have you plans in place for when the unthinkable happens, such as fires, floods, bombs, gas leaks, violence and so on. Obviously, by its nature, we cannot plan for the unexpected, but we can have in place plans for evacuation of the school and other emergency actions.

7   **Do you have a clear policy for contact with the media?** Every school wants to celebrate its achievements and it is a good idea to have someone who is responsible for remembering to let the world know about your successes. On the other hand, great damage can be done to a school's image if bad publicity is mismanaged. Are staff briefed on what it is sensible for them to communicate direct to the media and what they should refer upwards?

8   **Are your monitoring systems in place?** Are there people delegated to ensure that everything people said they would do is on target for completion by the deadlines? If commitments are made for improvements from one year to a next, are there systems to check back and evaluate progress? Is there a sense of purpose towards continuous improvement?

9   **Have you left room for the creative, off-the-wall elements that make individual schools special?** It would be a great shame if the system of planning and review made no space for those inspirational occasions that mark schools out individually.

10   **Do you have an annual cycle for school review?** Are staff clear about deadlines for planning documentation and is there a calendar available of the process of review, so that everyone knows what they should be doing when? Does this lead into a year-on-year programme of continuous review which allows channels for the continuous appraisal and modification of targets in the light of new data? School improvement must be an ongoing, cyclical and continuous process.

Conclusion

School improvement is a continuous process, but a book has to end somewhere. There are 500 tips here and readers who have got this far can probably think of at least another 500. You may well be thinking, 'But they haven't covered...' and 'There's not much about...', but we hope you will also be thinking, 'I liked the section on...', 'I wish I'd read this book before I started...', and 'I learned a lot about...'.

If any of these are true for you, we'd love to hear from you since, in keeping with the theme of this book, we aim to continuously improve our writing. Every book we write receives lots of feedback at a pilot stage from a number of other active practitioners, including, in this instance, inspectors, headteachers, trainers and classroom teachers, and we incorporate them into the final version. We also take note of all feedback we receive after publication and aim to use this advice to help us write the next edition or the next book. If you would like to join in, you can contact us via the publishers, Kogan Page, who will pass your comments on to us.

References And Useful Sources

Bradley, H (1991) *Staff Development*, School Development and Management of Change Series, Falmer Press, London.

Brown, S, Earlam, C and Race, P (1995) *500 Tips for Teachers*, Kogan Page, London.

Haines, C (1996) *School Improvement: Practical Strategies to Enhance Teaching and Learning*, Folems, London.

Hopkins, D, Ainscow, M and West, M (1994) *School Development in an Era of Change*, School Development Series, Cassell, London.

Horne, H and Pierce, A (1996) *A Practical Guide to Staff Development and Appraisal in Schools*, Kogan Page, London.

Kyriacou, C (1991) *Essential Teaching Skills*, Blackwell, Oxford.

Office for Standards in Education (OFSTED)(1996) *Subjects and Standards KS3, KS4 and Post 16*, HMSO, London.

OFSTED/Department for Education and Employment (DfEE)(1996) *Setting Targets to Improve Standards*, HMSO, London.

Porter, A C and Brophy, J E (1998) 'Synthesis of Research on Good Teaching: Insights from the Institute of Research on Teaching', *Educational Leadership*, 48(8), 74–85,

Race, P and McDowell, S (1996) *500 Computing Tips for Teachers and Lecturers*, Kogan Page, London.

Sutton, R (1994) *Assessment: A Framework for Teachers*, Routledge, London.

Index